A Complete
How-to Guide

Robert P. Kendall

THOMAS NELSON PUBLISHERS
Nashville

Library of Congress Cataloging-in-Publication Data

Kendall, Robert P.
  Getting the most from your New Strong's concordance / Robert P. Kendall.
    p. cm.
  ISBN 0-7852-4488-3
  1. Strong, James, 1822-1894. New exhaustive concordance of the Bible—Handbooks, manuals, etc. I. Strong, James, 1822-1894. New exhaustive concordance of the Bible. II. Title.

BS429.K46 2000
220.5'2033--dc21   99-462040

Printed in the United States of America

1 2 3 4 5 6 7—04 03 02 01 00

Contents

Introduction

Welcome to an adventure into the world of words. If you are like me, you have a longing to understand the Bible. You may have purchased some study helps—a study Bible, a couple of devotional books, and maybe even a concordance. If you do own a concordance, chances are that it is a *Strong's.*

I purchased a copy of *Strong's Exhaustive Concordance* years ago. I soon figured out how to find a verse in the Bible and how to look up a simple Greek or Hebrew word definition in the back of the book. But it was several years before I opened it with serious intent and began reading the study helps. With these helps I took my first steps into what has evolved into a daily study of the Bible with this great reference tool compiled by James Strong and first published more than one hundred years ago.

Looking up Bible verses with *Strong's* is the most basic use of the book. But you can also use it to do research into the Hebrew and Greek words that stand behind our English translations. *Strong's* is also a valuable tool when used with other Bible study aids such as Bible handbooks, general Bible dictionaries, and expository dictionaries.

I am writing this guide for the many people who have asked me Bible questions and were thrilled when I could show them how to find the answers on their own using their concordance. It is my desire to pass along to you, an owner—or prospective owner—of *Strong's Exhaustive Concordance,* some simple ways to get the most from your copy of this valuable Bible study tool.

About *Strong's Exhaustive Concordance*

The English word *concordance* comes from the Latin term *concordare*, which means "to agree." Thus, a concordance is a collection of passages which are similar in some way, or which agree with one another in some respect.

The main purpose of a biblical concordance is to help the reader find specific passages of Scripture. It does this by arranging all passages of the Bible under key words that the Bible student is likely to remember. By searching through all passages of the Bible which contain a specific key word, the reader is directed to the passage that he or she is seeking. Thus, a concordance is a valuable aid to systematic study of the Bible.

The first English concordance of the complete Bible was compiled in the 1500s by John Marbeck. This was followed by *Cruden's Concordance* (1737) and *Walker's Comprehensive Concordance* and *Young's Analytical Concordance* in the 1800s. The *Cruden's* and *Young's* concordances continue to have a limited following and are still being published.

But the concordance that won the day and that has remained immensely popular for more than one hundred years is *Strong's Exhaustive Concordance,* first published in 1890. It was compiled laboriously by hand over a period of thirty-five years under the supervision of Dr. James Strong (1822–1894), a linguist, Bible scholar, and professor of exegetical theology at Drew Theological Seminary in Madison, New Jersey.

The *Dictionary of American Biography* offers the following assessment of Strong's character as well as his contribution to biblical studies:

> Strong's great enthusiasm was the interpretation of the Bible, to which he brought independence of judgment and immense learning, including a profound knowledge of Greek, Hebrew, and the other Semitic languages. He traveled extensively in the Orient and acquainted himself with the latest developments in archeological research. He was also at home in the French and German literature pertaining to this field. His position was conservative: he stoutly defended the Mosaic authorship of the Pentateuch and the accuracy of the Mosaic account of creation, contended that there was but one Isaiah, and supported the Pauline authorship of the Epistle to the Hebrews; in all this, however, he was actuated not by blind obedience to the traditional, but by conviction based on his own studies.

REASONS FOR THE POPULARITY OF *STRONG'S*

There are five reasons why *Strong's* has become the most popular concordance in use today.

1. *The historical setting.* Because of the influence of Charles Darwin [1858] in the late 1800s, students of God's Word desired not only to find a word in the Bible but to understand it fully as well. Having their beliefs shaken by evolution and superior liberal scholarship, they were driven to seek a sure foundation. Liberal scholars held sway, as they could consult the original languages and put down the common person, who was not able to deal with such scholarship. *Strong's Concordance* offered easy access to the original languages in which the Bible was written.

2. *The Holy Spirit's original language choice.* Many students of God's Word are ignorant of the fact that it was originally written in Hebrew and Greek. Upon discovering this truth, they have a desire to be able to read these languages. *Strong's Concordance* was designed to help students do research into the Greek and Hebrew words behind the words used in the English-language King James Version of the Bible.

3. *More helpers and fewer mistakes.* The earlier editions of *Cruden's, Walker's,* and *Young's* were printed with mistakes, errors that were corrected in later editions. James Strong employed hundreds of helpers in his work. This resulted in a remarkably accurate concordance, even in the first printing.

4. *An exhaustive approach. Strong's* is an *exhaustive* concordance, meaning that every significant word in the English Bible is included. The only words not included as key words in his concordance were forty-seven that he classified as insignificant—articles and prepositions such as "a," "an," "the," and "that."

5. *A defense against liberalism. Strong's Concordance* served as a defense against liberal attacks upon the Bible. These went beyond the evolution issue to questions concerning inerrancy, authorship, the words of Jesus, and Jesus' virgin birth. *Strong's* gave non-scholars access to the scholar's material—material previously out of reach of the common person.

FEATURES OF *STRONG'S EXHAUSTIVE CONCORDANCE*

The first edition of James Strong's concordance contained these six features:

(1) the main concordance, all the significant words of the King James Version arranged alphabetically, with the Bible verses where these words occur;

(2) an addendum, containing words previously overlooked;

(3) an appendix of forty-seven insignificant words ("a," "an," "the," etc.);

(4) a comparative concordance, comparing the King James Version with the Revised English Version;

(5) a Hebrew dictionary, coded to English words by a Hebrew word numbering system; and

(6) a Greek dictionary, also coded to English words by a Greek word numbering system.

With repeated reprintings of this concordance over the years, some of these features have been dropped by various publishers. Other editions of *Strong's* have included supplements not contained in the original edition. But the four features of *Strong's* that have remained constant are: (1) the main concordance, (2) the appendix of insignificant words, (3) the Hebrew dictionary, and (4) the Greek dictionary. Here are reproductions of pages from a recent Thomas Nelson edition of *Strong's* that highlight these four abiding features of this concordance.

1. Main Concordance

ABOMINATIONS   9   **ABRAHAM**   **A**

weights are an a unto the LORD	Prov 20:23	8441
The sacrifice of the wicked is a	Prov 21:27	8441
and the scorner is an a to men	Prov 24:9	8441
law, even his prayer shall be a	Prov 28:9	8441
An unjust man is an a to the just	Prov 29:27	8441
in the way is a to the wicked	Prov 29:27	8441
incense is an a unto me	Is 1:13	8441
an a is he that chooseth you	Is 41:24	8441
I make the residue thereof an a	Is 44:19	8441
eating swine's flesh, and the a	Is 66:17	8263
land, and made mine heritage an a	Jer 2:7	8441
ashamed when they had committed a	Jer 6:15	8441
ashamed when they had committed a	Jer 8:12	8441
mind, that they should do this a	Jer 32:35	8441
haughty, and committed a before me	Eze 16:50	8441
to the idols, hath committed a	Eze 18:12	8441
one hath committed a with his	Eze 22:11	8441
stand upon your sword, ye work a	Eze 33:26	8441
place the a that maketh desolate	Dan 11:31	8251
the a that maketh desolate set up	Dan 12:11	8251
an a is committed in Israel and in	Mal 2:11	8441
shall see the a of desolation	Mt 24:15	946
ye shall see the a of desolation	Mk 13:14	946
men is a in the sight of God	Lk 16:15	946
neither whatsoever worketh a	Rev 21:27	946

ABOMINATIONS

shall not commit any of these a	Lev 18:26	8441
(For all these a have the men of	Lev 18:27	8441
shall commit any of these a	Lev 18:29	8441
do after the a of those nations	Deut 18:9	8441
because of these a the LORD thy	Deut 18:12	8441
you not to do after all their a	Deut 20:18	8441
And ye have seen their a, and their	Deut 29:17	8251
with a provoked they him to anger	Deut 32:16	8441
a of the nations which the LORD	1Kin 14:24	8441
according to the a of the heathen	2Kin 16:3	8441
after the a of the heathen, whom	2Kin 21:2	8441
king of Judah hath done these a	2Kin 21:11	8441
all the a that were spied in the	2Kin 23:24	8251
after the a of the heathen whom	2Chr 28:3	8441
like unto the a of the heathen,	2Chr 33:2	8441
Josiah took away all the a out of	2Chr 34:33	8441
his a which he did, and that which	2Chr 36:8	8441
after all the a of the heathen	2Chr 36:14	8441
lands, doing according to their a	Ezr 9:1	8441
people of the lands, with their a	Ezr 9:11	8441
with the people of these a	Ezr 9:14	8441
there are seven a in his heart	Prov 26:25	8441
their soul delighteth in their a	Is 66:3	8251
put away their a out of my sight	Jer 4:1	8251
are delivered to do all these a	Jer 7:10	8441
they have set their a in the	Jer 7:30	8251
thine a on the hills in the	Jer 13:27	8251
But they set their a in the house	Jer 32:34	8251
because of the a which ye have	Jer 44:22	8441
the like, because of all thine a	Eze 5:9	8441
things, and will all thine a	Eze 5:11	8441
have committed in all their a	Eze 6:9	8441
Alas for all the evil a of the	Eze 6:11	8441
recompense upon thee all thine a	Eze 7:3	8441
thine a shall be in the midst of	Eze 7:4	8441
recompense thee for all thine a	Eze 7:8	8441
thine a that are in the midst of	Eze 7:9	8441
they made the images of their a	Eze 7:20	8441
even the great a that the house	Eze 8:6	8441
and thou shalt see greater a	Eze 8:6	8441
the wicked a that they do here	Eze 8:9	8441
shalt see greater a that they do	Eze 8:13	8441
shalt see greater a than these	Eze 8:15	8441
the a which they commit here	Eze 8:17	8441
that cry for all the a that be	Eze 9:4	8441
all the a thereof from thence	Eze 11:18	8441
detestable things and their a	Eze 11:21	8441
a among the heathen whither they	Eze 12:16	8441
away your faces from all your a	Eze 14:6	8441
cause Jerusalem to know her a	Eze 16:2	8441
And in all thine a and thy	Eze 16:22	8441
and with all the idols of thy a	Eze 16:36	8441
this lewdness above all thine a	Eze 16:43	8441
ways, nor done after their a	Eze 16:47	8441
multiplied thine a more than they	Eze 16:51	8441
all thine a which thou hast done	Eze 16:51	8441
borne thy lewdness and thine a	Eze 16:58	8441
he hath done all these a	Eze 18:13	8441
the a that the wicked man doeth	Eze 18:24	8441
to know the a of their fathers	Eze 20:4	8441
away every man the a of his eyes	Eze 20:7	8251
man cast away the a of their eyes	Eze 20:8	8251
commit ye whoredom after their a	Eze 20:30	8251
thou shalt shew her all her a	Eze 22:2	8441

yea, declare unto them their a	Eze 23:36	8441
their a which they have committed	Eze 33:29	8441
for your iniquities and for your a	Eze 36:31	8441
their a that they have committed	Eze 43:8	8441
let it suffice you of all your a	Eze 44:6	8441
my covenant because of all your a	Eze 44:7	8441
their a which they have committed	Eze 44:13	8441
for the overspreading of a he	Dan 9:27	8251
their a were according as they	Hos 9:10	8251
his a from between his teeth	Zec 9:7	8251
golden cup in her hand full of a	Rev 17:4	946
AND A OF THE EARTH	Rev 17:5	946

ABOUND

man shall a with blessings	Prov 28:20	7227
And because iniquity shall a	Mt 24:12	4129
entered, that the offence might a	Rom 5:20	4121
abounded, grace did much more a	Rom 5:20	5248
continue in sin, that grace may a	Rom 6:1	4121
believing, that ye may a in hope	Rom 15:13	4052
the sufferings of Christ a in us	2Cor 1:5	4052
as ye a in every thing, in faith,	2Cor 8:7	4052
see that ye a in this grace also	2Cor 8:7	4052
to make all grace a toward you	2Cor 9:8	4052
things, may a to every good work	2Cor 9:8	4052
that your love may a yet more	Phil 1:9	4052
to be abased, and I know how to a	Phil 4:12	4052
full and to be hungry, both to a	Phil 4:12	4052
fruit that may a to your account	Phil 4:17	4121
But I have all, and a	Phil 4:18	4052
a in love one toward another, and	1Th 3:12	4052
to please God, so ye would a more	1Th 4:1	4052
if these things be in you, and a	2Pet 1:8	4121

ABOUNDED

a through my lie unto his glory	Rom 3:7	4052
Jesus Christ, hath a unto many	Rom 5:15	4052
But where sin a. grace did much	Rom 5:20	4121
their deep poverty a unto the	2Cor 8:2	4052
Wherein he hath a toward us in	Eph 1:8	4052

ABOUNDETH

a furious man a in transgression	Prov 29:22	7227
our consolation also a by Christ	2Cor 1:5	4052
of you all toward each other a	2Th 1:3	4121

ABOUNDING

were no fountains a with water	Prov 8:24	3513
always a in the work of the Lord,	1Cor 15:58	4052
a therein with thanksgiving	Col 2:7	4052

ABOUT See APPENDIX.

ABOVE See APPENDIX.

ABRAHAM (a'-bra-ham) See ABRAHAM'S, ABRAM. *Father of the nation of Israel.*

Abram, but thy name shall be A	Gen 17:5	85
And God said unto A, Thou shalt	Gen 17:9	85
And God said unto A, As for Sarai	Gen 17:15	85
Then A fell upon his face, and	Gen 17:17	85
A said unto God, O that Ishmael	Gen 17:18	85
with him, and God went up from A	Gen 17:22	85
A took Ishmael his son, and all	Gen 17:23	85
A was ninety years old and nine	Gen 17:24	85
selfsame day was A circumcised	Gen 17:26	85
A hastened into the tent unto	Gen 18:6	85
A ran unto the herd, and fetch a	Gen 18:7	85
Now A and Sarah were old and well	Gen 18:11	85
And the LORD said unto A,	Gen 18:13	85
A went with them to bring them on	Gen 18:16	85
Shall I hide from A that thing	Gen 18:17	85
Seeing that A shall surely become	Gen 18:18	85
A that which he hath spoken of	Gen 18:19	85
but A stood yet before the LORD	Gen 18:22	85
A drew near, and said, Wilt thou	Gen 18:23	85
A answered and said, Behold now, I	Gen 18:27	85
as he had left communing with A	Gen 18:33	85
A returned unto his place	Gen 18:33	85
A gat up early in the morning to	Gen 19:27	85
the plain, that God remembered A	Gen 19:29	85
A journeyed from thence toward	Gen 20:1	85
A said of Sarah his wife, She is	Gen 20:2	85
Then Abimelech called A, and said	Gen 20:9	85
And Abimelech said unto A, What	Gen 20:10	85
A said, Because I thought, Surely	Gen 20:11	85
and gave them unto A, and restored	Gen 20:14	85
So A prayed unto God	Gen 20:17	85
bare A a son in his old age, at	Gen 21:2	85
A called the name of his son that	Gen 21:3	85
A circumcised his son Isaac being	Gen 21:4	85
A was an hundred years old, when	Gen 21:5	85
said, Who would have said unto A	Gen 21:7	85
A made a great feast the same day	Gen 21:8	85

2. Appendix of Insignificant Words

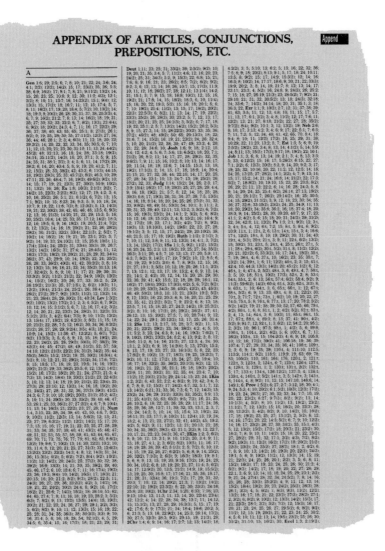

3. Hebrew Dictionary

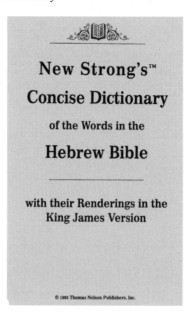

4. Greek Dictionary

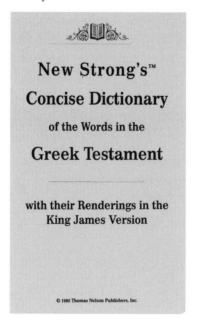

MODERN EDITIONS OF *STRONG'S*

Strong's Exhaustive Concordance is being issued today by several different publishers, including Abingdon Press, Hendrickson Publishers, Thomas Nelson, and World. Nelson's commitment to *Strong's* goes back to 1984, when it issued the concordance in a new typesetting and with several other enhancements. Because of these improvements, Nelson refers to its editions as the *New Strong's*™ *Exhaustive Concordance.* Five different editions of *Strong's* have been published under the *New Strong's*™ label. Here's a description of these five and their distinctive features.

The New Strong's™ Exhaustive Concordance of the Bible (1984)

- Main concordance, keyed to Strong's numbering system

- Hebrew and Greek dictionaries

- Appendix of 47 insignificant words

- New computer-generated typesetting

- Hebrew and Greek reference numbers placed next to the Scripture citation for easy reference

- Proper names from other translations besides KJV added as cross-references

(Out of print)

- Proper names that refer to more than one person divided into separate entries

- Key verse comparison chart (1,800 verses, 6 versions)

- A few supplements

The New Strong's™ Exhaustive Concordance of the Bible (1990)

- Main concordance, keyed to Strong's numbering system

- Hebrew and Greek dictionaries

- Proper names from other translations besides KJV listed as cross-references

- Appendix of 47 insignificant words

- Fan-Tab™ thumb-index reference system added

- Topical index to the Bible added

- Words of Christ in main concordance highlighted by shading

- Numerous supplements added

- Corrections of 1984 edition

- Improved design and format

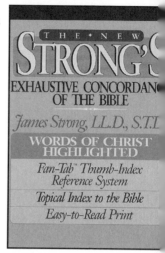

The New Strong's™ Exhaustive Concordance of the Bible (Comfort Print Edition) (1995)

- Main concordance, keyed to Strong's numbering system

- Hebrew and Greek dictionaries

- Proper names from other translations besides KJV listed as cross-references

- Total book, including Hebrew and Greek dictionaries, re-typeset in larger, easier-to-read print

- Appendix of insignificant words expanded and reformatted for easier use

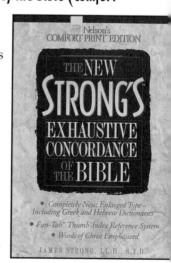

- Hebrew and Greek dictionaries updated, using consistent abbreviations throughout, adding variant readings, and adding reader-friendly introductions on how to use the Hebrew and Greek dictionaries

- Words of Christ in main concordance appear in boldface type

- Fan-Tab™ thumb-index reference system

The New Strong's™ Exhaustive Concordance of the Bible (Super Value Edition) (1995, 1996)

- Main concordance, keyed to Strong's numbering system

- Hebrew and Greek dictionaries

- Expanded appendix of insignificant words

- Published in compact size, 6⅜" x 9¼"

- Words of Christ in main concordance in boldface type

- Fan-Tab™ thumb-index reference system

The New Strong's™ Concise Concordance of the Bible

- Main concordance

- Eliminates appendix of insignificant words

- Published in concise size, 6⅜" x 9¼"

- Words of Christ in main concordance in boldface type

- Fan-Tab™ thumb-index reference system

Using *Strong's* to Find a Specific Verse in the Bible

Every Bible student has those times when he needs to find a specific verse but doesn't know where it occurs in the Bible. Your *Strong's* can help in this situation.

Let's assume you are studying your Bible in preparation for teaching a Sunday school lesson on discipleship. You want to emphasize the need for believers to be led by the spirit of Christ and not be overly influenced by the surrounding culture. You recall that Paul had something to say about a Christian's need to be "transformed" by the spirit of Christ.

You look under <u>transformed</u> in the main concordance section of *Strong's*—and there's the verse you're looking for:

TRANSFIGURED			1375
TRANSFIGURED			
And was *t* before them	Mt 17:2	3339	
and he was *t* before them	Mk 9:2	3339	
TRANSFORMED			
but be ye *t* by the renewing of	Rom 12:2	3339	
for Satan himself is *t* into an	2Cor 11:14	3345	
also be *t* as the ministers of	2Cor 11:15	3345	
TRANSFORMING			
t themselves into the apostles of	2Cor 11:13	3345	

Now that *Strong's* has helped you find the right verse, you can go to your Bible to find the full passage with its context: "And be not conformed to this world: but be ye transformed by the renewing of your mind, that ye may prove what is that good, and acceptable, and perfect, will of God."

Not every verse you are trying to locate will be this easy to find, of course. Some words in *Strong's Concordance* have hundreds of entries. For example, the word <u>servant</u> occurs more than five hundred times in the King James Bible. Let's assume you are looking for the verse where a Roman centurion asked Jesus to heal his servant. If you look under <u>servant</u>, you will probably have a difficult time locating the specific verse. But if you look under <u>centurion</u> and/or <u>centurion's</u>, you will find the verse easily:

...ns, and u.		
b...uns, and the spoo..., .		
CENTURION		
there came unto him a *c*,	Mt 8:5	1543
The *c* answered and said, Lord, I	Mt 8:8	1543
And Jesus said unto the *c*, Go thy	Mt 8:13	1543
Now when the *c*, and they that were	Mt 27:54	1543
And when the *c*, which stood over	Mk 15:39	2760
and calling unto him the *c*	Mk 15:44	2760
And when he knew it of the *c*	Mk 15:45	2760
the *c* sent friends to him, saying	Lk 7:6	1543
Now when the *c* saw what was done,	Lk 23:47	1543
a *c* of the band called the	Acts 10:1	1543
And they said, Cornelius the *c*	Acts 10:22	1543
said unto the *c* that stood by	Acts 22:25	1543
When the *c* heard that, he went and	Acts 22:26	1543
And he commanded a *c* to keep Paul	Acts 24:23	1543
Julius, a *c* of Augustus' band	Acts 27:1	1543
there the *c* found a ship of	Acts 27:6	1543
Nevertheless the *c* believed the	Acts 27:11	1543
Paul said to the *c* and to the	Acts 27:31	1543
But the *c*, willing to save Paul,	Acts 27:43	1543
the *c* delivered the prisoners to	Acts 28:16	1543
CENTURION'S		
And a certain *c* servant, who was	Lk 7:2	1543
CENTURIONS		
immediately took soldiers and *c*	Acts 21:32	1543
Paul called one of the *c* unto him	Acts 23:17	1543
And he called unto him two *c*	Acts 23:23	1543

If you can't find the verse you are looking for under one word, try to think of other words from the same verse that will yield a successful search.

Let's pursue this principle by trying to find the same verse under several different key words. Assume you remember that there is a beautiful benediction from the Bible with the words, "To him who is able to keep us from falling." You would like to use this in a public prayer, but you don't know where to find the complete verse. You decide to look under <u>able</u>, <u>keep</u>, and <u>falling</u> in *Strong's*.

Both <u>able</u> and <u>keep</u> have scores of entries—too many to search through. But <u>falling</u> gives you what you're looking for at a glance·

Another good way to use *Strong's* is to search for every occurrence of a specific English word in the Bible. For example, let's assume you want to prepare a devotional meditation on the theme of thanksgiving. You need to search the Bible for specific mentions of the theme of giving thanks to God.

When you turn to the main concordance section of *Strong's*, you

grass, and the flower thereof *f*	Jas 1:11	1601
and the flower thereof *f* away	1Pet 1:24	1601
FALLING		
f into a trance, but having his	Num 24:4	5307
f into a trance, but having his	Num 24:16	5307
have upholden him that was *f*	Job 4:4	3782
the mountain *f* cometh to nought	Job 14:18	5307
not thou deliver my feet from *f*	Ps 56:13	1762
from tears, and my feet from *f*	Ps 116:8	1762
A righteous man *f* down before the	Prov 25:26	4131
as a *f* fig from the fig tree	Is 34:4	5034
f down before him, she declared	Lk 8:47	4363
of blood *f* down to the ground	Lk 22:44	2597
f headlong, he burst asunder in	Acts 1:18	4248,1096
f into a place where two seas met	Acts 27:41	4045
so *f* down on his face he will	1Cor 14:25	4098
except there come a *f* away first	2Th 2:3	646
that is able to keep you from *f*	Jude 24	679
FALLOW		
the *f* deer, and the wild goat, and	Deut 14:5	3180

immediately notice three words on the theme of giving thanks: <u>thanks</u>, <u>thanksgiving</u>, and <u>thanksgivings</u>. (See page 15.)

You notice that the psalms are particularly rich in their expression of thanks to God. The word <u>thanks</u> appears twenty-three times in the psalms, and the word <u>thanksgiving</u> appears eight times in this Old Testament book.

With this information, you decide to use Psalm 136 as the basis for your meditation on thanksgiving. The phrase "O give thanks unto the Lord" or "O give thanks unto God" appears four times in this psalm: in verses 1, 2, 3, and 26. It's an ideal text to use to call Christians to express their thanks to God for His many bountiful gifts.

Strong's is also an excellent resource for doing research on a verse-by-verse basis on particular places or people in the Bible. For example, let's assume you are preparing a Bible study lesson on Moses. You turn to the entry on <u>Moses</u> in the main concordance section of *Strong's.* You are struck with the hundreds of references to Moses in Exodus, Leviticus, Numbers, and Deuteronomy. These books cover the years when Moses was leading the Israelites out of Egyptian slavery and guiding them during the wilderness wandering years.

But you also find that Moses is mentioned hundreds of times throughout the rest of the Old Testament. Even in the New Testament his name is mentioned dozens of times. Doing further research by reading these individual verses where Moses is

THAMAR	1349	THEE

THAMAR (tha'-mar) See TAMAR. *Mother of Phares and Zara; ancestor of Jesus.*
Judas begat Phares and Zara of *T* .... Mt 1:3 — 2283

THAN See APPENDIX.

THANK
the LORD, and to record, and to *t* .... 1Chr 16:4 — 3034
delivered first this psalm to *t* .... 1Chr 16:7 — 3034
And to stand every morning to *t* .... 1Chr 23:30 — 3034
we *t* thee, and praise thy glorious .... 1Chr 29:13 — 3034
t offerings into the house of the .... 2Chr 29:31 — 8426
in sacrifices and *t* offerings .... 2Chr 29:31 — 8426
t offerings, and commanded Judah .... 2Chr 33:16 — 8426
I *t* thee, and praise thee, O thou .... Dan 2:23 — 3029
I *t* thee, O Father, Lord of .... Mt 11:25 — 1843
which love you, what *t* have ye .... Lk 6:32 — 5485
do good to you, what *t* have ye .... Lk 6:33 — 5485
hope to receive, what *t* have ye .... Lk 6:34 — 5485
I *t* thee, O Father, Lord of .... Lk 10:21 — 1843
Doth he *t* that servant because he . Lk 17:9 — 2192,5485
I *t* thee, that I am not as other .... Lk 18:11 — 2168
I *t* thee that thou hast heard me .... Jn 11:41 — 2168
I *t* my God through Jesus Christ .... Rom 1:8 — 2168
I *t* God through Jesus Christ our .... Rom 7:25 — 2168
I *t* my God always on your behalf, ... 1Cor 1:4 — 2168
I *t* God that I baptized none of .... 1Cor 1:14 — 2168
I *t* my God, I speak with tongues .... 1Cor 14:18 — 2168
I *t* my God upon every remembrance .. Phil 1:3 — 2168
For this cause also *t* we God .... 1Th 2:13 — 3670
We are bound to *t* God always for ... 2Th 1:3 — 2168
I *t* Christ Jesus our Lord, who ...... 1Ti 1:12 — 2192,5485
I *t* God, whom I serve from my ...... 2Ti 1:3 — 2192,5485
I *t* my God, making mention of .... Philem 4 — 2168

THANKED
and bowed himself, and *t* the king .... 2Sa 14:22 — 1288
he *t* God, and took courage .... Acts 28:15 — 2168
But God be *t*, that ye were the .... Rom 6:17 — 5485

THANKFUL
be *t* unto him, and bless his name........ Ps 100:4 — 3034
him not as God, neither were *t* .... Rom 1:21 — 2168
and be ye *t* .... Col 3:15 — 2170

THANKFULNESS
most noble Felix, with all *t* .... Acts 24:3 — 2169

THANKING
heard in praising and *t* the LORD .... 2Chr 5:13 — 3034

THANKS
Therefore I will give *t* unto thee .... 2Sa 22:50 — 3034
Give *t* unto the LORD, call upon .... 1Chr 16:8 — 3034
O give *t* unto the LORD .... 1Chr 16:34 — 3034
we may give *t* to thy holy name .... 1Chr 16:35 — 3034
to give *t* to the LORD, because .... 1Chr 16:41 — 3034
prophesied with a harp, to give *t* .... 1Chr 25:3 — 3034
to minister, and to give *t* .... 2Chr 31:2 — 3034
and giving *t* unto the LORD .... Ezr 3:11 — 3034
them, to praise and to give *t* .... Neh 12:24 — 3034
companies of them that gave *t* .... Neh 12:31 — 8426
gave *t* went over against them .... Neh 12:38 — 8426
that gave *t* in the house of God .... Neh 12:40 — 8426
the grave who shall give thee *t* .... Ps 6:5 — 3034
Therefore will I give *t* unto thee .... Ps 18:49 — 3034
give *t* at the remembrance of his .... Ps 30:4 — 3034
I will give *t* unto thee for ever .... Ps 30:12 — 3034
I will give thee *t* in the great .... Ps 35:18 — 3034
Unto thee, O God, do we give *t* .... Ps 75:1 — 3034
unto thee do we give *t* .... Ps 75:1 — 3034
pasture will give thee *t* for ever .... Ps 79:13 — 3034
thing to give *t* unto the LORD .... Ps 92:1 — 3034
give *t* at the remembrance of his .... Ps 97:12 — 3034
O give *t* unto the LORD .... Ps 105:1 — 3034
O give *t* unto the LORD .... Ps 106:1 — 3034
to give *t* unto thy holy name, and .... Ps 106:47 — 3034
O give *t* unto the LORD, for he is .... Ps 107:1 — 3034
O give *t* unto the LORD .... Ps 118:1 — 3034
O give *t* unto the LORD .... Ps 118:29 — 3034
give *t* unto thee because of thy .... Ps 119:62 — 3034
to give *t* unto the name of the .... Ps 122:4 — 3034
O Give *t* unto the LORD .... Ps 136:1 — 3034
O give *t* unto the God of gods .... Ps 136:2 — 3034
O give *t* to the Lord of lords .... Ps 136:3 — 3034
O give *t* unto the God of heaven .... Ps 136:26 — 3034
shall give *t* unto thy name .... Ps 140:13 — 3034
gave *t* before his God, as he did .... Dan 6:10 — 3029
loaves and the fishes, and gave *t* .... Mt 15:36 — 2168
And he took the cup, and gave *t* .... Mt 26:27 — 2168
took the seven loaves, and gave *t* .... Mk 8:6 — 2168
the cup, and when he had given *t*, ... Mk 14:23 — 2168
gave *t* likewise unto the Lord .... Lk 2:38 — 437
___ _ giving him *t* .... Lk 17:16 — 2168

And he took the cup, and gave *t* .... Lk 22:17 — 2168
And he took bread, and gave *t* .... Lk 22:19 — 2168
and when he had given *t*, he .... Jn 6:11 — 2168
after that the Lord had given *t* .... Jn 6:23 — 2168
gave *t* to God in presence of them........ Acts 27:35 — 2168
to the Lord, for he giveth God *t* .... Rom 14:6 — 2168
he eateth not, and giveth God *t* .... Rom 14:6 — 2168
unto whom not only I give *t* .... Rom 16:4 — 2168
of for that for which I give *t* .... 1Cor 10:30 — 2168
And when he had given *t*, he brake ...... 1Cor 11:24 — 2168
say Amen at thy giving of *t* .... 1Cor 14:16 — 2169
For thou verily givest *t* well .... 1Cor 14:17 — 2168
But *t* be to God, which giveth us .... 1Cor 15:57 — 5485
I may be given by many on our .... 2Cor 1:11 — 2168
Now *t* be unto God, which always .... 2Cor 2:14 — 5485
But *t* be to God, which put the .... 2Cor 8:16 — 5485
T be unto God for his unspeakable .... 2Cor 9:15 — 5485
Cease not to give *t* for you .... Eph 1:16 — 2168
but rather giving of *t* .... Eph 5:4 — 2169
Giving *t* always for all things .... Eph 5:20 — 2168
We give *t* to God and the Father of ...... Col 1:3 — 2168
Giving *t* unto the Father, which .... Col 1:12 — 2168
the Lord Jesus, giving *t* to God .... Col 3:17 — 2168
We give *t* to God always for you .... 1Th 1:2 — 2168
For what *t* can we render to God .... 1Th 3:9 — 2169
In every thing give *t* .... 1Th 5:18 — 2168
to give *t* alway to God for you .... 2Th 2:13 — 2168
intercessions, and giving of *t* .... 1Ti 2:1 — 2169
of our lips giving *t* to his name .... Heb 13:15 — 3670
t to him that sat on the throne, ... Rev 4:9 — 2169
Saying, We give thee *t*, O Lord .... Rev 11:17 — 2168

THANKSGIVING
If he offer it for a *t*, then he .... Lev 7:12 — 8426
offer with the sacrifice of *t* .... Lev 7:12 — 8426
of *t* of his peace offerings .... Lev 7:13 — 8426
of his peace offerings for *t* .... Lev 7:15 — 8426
a sacrifice of *t* unto the LORD .... Lev 22:29 — 8426
to begin the *t* in prayer .... Neh 11:17 — 3034
Mattaniah, which was over the *t* .... Neh 12:8 — 1960
and songs of praise and *t* unto God ...... Neh 12:46 — 8426
I may publish with the voice of *t* .... Ps 26:7 — 3034
Offer unto God *t* .... Ps 50:14 — 8426
and will magnify him with *t* .... Ps 69:30 — 8426
come before his presence with *t* .... Ps 95:2 — 8426
Enter into his gates with *t* .... Ps 100:4 — 8426
sacrifice the sacrifices of *t* .... Ps 107:22 — 8426
offer to thee the sacrifice of *t* .... Ps 116:17 — 8426
Sing unto the LORD with *t* .... Ps 147:7 — 8426
shall be found therein, *t* .... Is 51:3 — 8426
And out of them shall proceed *t* .... Jer 30:19 — 8426
a sacrifice of *t* with leaven .... Amos 4:5 — 8426
unto thee with the voice of *t* .... Jonah 2:9 — 8426
grace might through the *t* of many ...... 2Cor 4:15 — 2169
which causeth through us *t* to God ...... 2Cor 9:11 — 2169
supplication with *t* let your .... Phil 4:6 — 2169
taught, abounding therein with *t* .... Col 2:7 — 2169
and watch in the same with *t* .... Col 4:2 — 2169
with *t* of them which believe .... 1Ti 4:3 — 2169
refused, if it be received with *t* .... 1Ti 4:4 — 2169
and glory, and wisdom, and *t* .... Rev 7:12 — 2169

THANKSGIVINGS
with gladness, both with *t* .... Neh 12:27 — 8426
abundant also by many *t* unto God ...... 2Cor 9:12 — 2169

THANKWORTHY
For this is *t*, if a man for .... 1Pet 2:19 — 5485

THARA (tha'-rah) See TERAH. *Greek form of Terah.*
Abraham, which was the son of *T* .... Lk 3:34 — 2291

THARSHISH (thar'-shish) See TARSHISH.
1. *Ships fitted for long voyages.*
navy of *T* with the navy of Hiram........ 1Kin 10:22 — 8659
in three years came the navy of *T* ...... 1Kin 22:48 — 8659
of *T* to go to Ophir for gold............ 1Kin 22:48 — 8659
2. *Son of Bilhan.*
and Chenaanah, and Zethan, and *T* .. 1Chr 7:10 — 8659

THAT See APPENDIX.

THE See APPENDIX.

THEATRE
rushed with one accord into the *t* .... Acts 19:29 — 2302
not adventure himself into the *t* .... Acts 19:31 — 2302

THEBES See THEBEZ.

THEBEZ (the'-bez) *A city in Ephraim.*
Then went Abimelech to *T*, and .... Judg 9:50 — 8405
to *T*, and encamped against *T* .... Judg 9:50 — 8405
from the wall, that he died in *T* .... 2Sa 11:21 — 8405

THEE See APPENDIX.

T

mentioned will give you greater insight into the life and character of this great leader in the history of Israel.

One problem to be aware of in using *Strong's* for verse searching is the different phraseology used by various translations of the Bible. *Strong's* is based on the words used in the King James Version. These words may or may not match the words used in more modern translations such as the NIV and the NRSV. When using *Strong's*, you need to try to think in "King James English." For example, ask yourself how the concepts, words, and ideas from the NIV would probably be expressed in the KJV. This might give you a clue about the key word to look under in *Strong's*.

All editions of *Strong's Exhaustive Concordance* published by Thomas Nelson since 1984 have addressed this word variation problem to some extent by publishing variant proper names from other translations as cross-references to the appropriate KJV name that appears in *Strong's*. For example, the KJV word <u>Accad</u> is rendered as <u>Akkad</u> by the NIV. In Nelson's *Strong's* at the entry word <u>Akkad</u>, the reader is directed to <u>Accad</u>.

> ..... onaalabbin, a.....
>   *3. A town between Benjamin and Judah.*
>   and had taken Beth-shemesh, and *A* 2Chr 28:18   357
> **AKAN** *(a'-kan)* See JAAKAN, JAKAN. *A son of Ezer.*
>   Bilhan, and Zaavan, and *A* .... Gen 36:27   6130
> **AKEL DAMA** See ACELDAMA.
> **AKKAD** See ACCAD.
> **AKKUB** *(ak'-kub)*
>   *1. A descendant of David.*
>   and Eliashib, and Pelaiah, and *A* 1Chr 3:24   6126
>   *2. A Levitical gatekeeper.*
>   the porters were, Shallum, and *A* 1Chr 9:17   6126
>   Moreover the porters, *A*, Talmon, ... Neh 11:19   6126
>   Obadiah, Meshullam, Talmon, *A* .... Neh 12:25   61⁻

Using *Strong's* for Basic Word Studies

I f you are using *Strong's* for nothing but finding verses, you are missing out on a lot of exciting Bible study. This chapter will lead you step by step through the process of getting at the meaning of the Hebrew and Greek words that were translated into English by the King James translators. You will be working with the Hebrew and Greek dictionaries at the back of your *Strong's Concordance,* conducting beginning, intermediate, and advanced word studies in each of these biblical languages.

HEBREW WORD STUDIES

1. A Simple Search: When the Hebrew Word Is a Primary Root

In this exercise you will learn to find the Hebrew root word behind an English word when the underlying Hebrew word is a primary root. These steps can be learned in one reading. Finding a verse, looking up a definition, and digging up the Hebrew root for a word are simple and straightforward. You will be relying on Strong's word definition plus the translated words as chosen by the King James translators.

In every entry in the Hebrew dictionary, Strong's definition of the word will be in italics and the KJV translations of the word will follow this sign (:-). You will simply find a definition by using

Strong's Concordance as a dictionary. So get your *Strong's* and follow along step by step, first reading what is in this book and then referring to your concordance.

Imagine that you are reading Proverbs 3:19, "The LORD by wisdom hath founded the earth; by understanding hath he established the heavens." You are interested in the verb *founded*. You want to know the meaning of the Hebrew behind the English. Follow these steps:

1. In the main concordance section of *Strong's*, look up <u>founded</u>. You find the Proverbs 3:19 entry, "LORD by wisdom hath *f* the earth   Prov 3:19   3245."

the wall of the city has		
the *f* of the wall of the city	Rev 21:19	2310
FOUNDED		
For he hath *f* it upon the seas,	Ps 24:2	3245
fulness thereof, thou hast *f* them	Ps 89:11	3245
place which thou hast *f* for them	Ps 104:8	3245
that thou hast *f* them for ever	Ps 119:152	3245
LORD by wisdom hath *f* the earth	Prov 3:19	3245
That the LORD hath *f* Zion	Is 14:32	3245
til the Assyrian *f* it for them	Is 23:13	3245
hath *f* his troop in the earth	Amos 9:6	3245
for it was *f* upon a rock	Mt 7:25	2311
for it was *f* upon a rock	Lk 6:48	2311
FOUNDER		
of silver ... ... to the *f*	Jude	

2. Note that Strong's number for the Hebrew word behind <u>founded</u> is 3245. Turn to the back of your *Strong's Concordance* to the Hebrew dictionary and find the word numbered 3245.

blowing ci....
heron is meant [comp. 5399]):— (great) owl.

3245. יָסַד **yâçad**, *yaw-sad'*; a prim. root; to *set* (lit. or fig.); intens. to *found*; refl. to *sit* down together, i.e. *settle*, *consult*:— appoint, take counsel, establish, (lay the, lay for a) found (-ation), instruct, lay, ordain, set, × sure.

3246. יְסֻד **y⁰çûd**, *yes-ood'*; from 3245; a *foundation* (fig. i.e. *beginning*):— × began.

3247. יְסוֹד **⁰côwd**, *yes-ode'*; from 3245

3. Here is an explanation of what you see under the word 3245:

- The number of the word is followed by the Hebrew word itself, its English transliteration, and its English pronunciation.

- The information between the English pronunciation and this symbol (:-) is the definition part of the entry. The designation "a prim. root" means that this Hebrew word is a primary root. The definitions that appear in italics give the various meanings of this word in Hebrew (to *found*, to *sit* down together, i.e. *settle, consult*).

- The different English words that were used by the King James translators to render the meaning of this word in English are listed after this symbol (:-). Note that the different words used include "appoint, take counsel, establish, (lay the, lay for a) found (-ation), instruct, lay, ordain, set, sure."

4. Now that you have discerned the Hebrew definition of this word, you can take the expanded facets of your English word <u>founded</u> and have a clearer picture of what it means for God to found the earth. Combine Strong's definition part of the entry with the KJV translators' translation part of the entry. Thus, the Hebrew word behind the English word can be understood as: "God by wisdom, appointed, ordained, set in order, laid the foundation for, established the earth."

2. An Intermediate Search: When the Hebrew Word Is from Another Root

In this exercise you will learn how to find the Hebrew root word behind an English word when the underlying Hebrew word is from another Hebrew root.

Let's assume that you are reading Job 21:34: "How then comfort ye me in vain, seeing in your answers there remaineth falsehood?" You are interested in the word *falsehood*. You want to know the meaning of the Hebrew behind this English term. Follow these steps:

1. In the main concordance section of *Strong's*, look up <u>false-hood</u>. You find the Job 21:34 entry: "in your answers there remaineth *f* Job 21:34   4604."

> w... mim the *f* propn...
> the *f* prophet are, and shall be .... Rev 20:10   5578
> **FALSEHOOD**
> wrought *f* against mine own life 2Sa 18:13   8267
> in your answers there remaineth *f*.......... Job 21:34   4604
> mischief, and brought forth *f*.................. Ps 7:14   8267
> for their deceit is *f*...................................... Ps 119:118   8267
> right hand is a right hand of *f*................. Ps 144:8   8267
> right hand is a right hand of *f*................. Ps 144:11   8267
> under *f* have we hid ourselves.................. Is 28:15   8267
> of transgression, a seed of *f*..................... Is 57:4   8267
> from the heart words of *f*.......................... Is 59:13   8267
> for his molten image is *f*........................... Jer 10:14   8267
> forgotten me, and trusted in *f*................. Jer 13:25   8267
> for his molten image is *f*........................... Jer 51:17   8267

2. Note that Strong's number for the Hebrew word behind <u>falsehood</u> is 4604. Turn to the back of your *Strong's Concordance* to the Hebrew dictionary and find the word numbered 4604.

> 4603. מָעַל **mâ'al**, *maw...*, *a prim...*.
> prop. *to cover* up; used only fig. *to act*
> *covertly*, i.e. *treacherously*:— trans-
> gress, (commit, do a) trespass (-ing).
>
> 4604. מַעַל **ma'al**, *mah´-al*; from 4603;
> *treachery*, i.e. *sin*:— falsehood, griev-
> ously, sore, transgression, trespass, ×
> very.
>
> 4605. מַעַל **ma'al**, *mah´al*; from 5927;
> prop. the *upper* part, used only adv.
> with pref. *upward*, *above*, *overhead*,
> *from the top*, etc.:— above, exceeding

3. Note that all the elements of this entry are the same as they were for the simple search for a Hebrew primary root which you have just conducted—with this exception: Word number 4604 is not a primary root, but it derives from word 4603, which is the primary root. Turn to this word.

> ...achnathites.
> 4602. מַעֲכָתִי **Ma'ăkâthîy**, *mah-ak-aw-
> thee´*; patrial from 4601; a *Maakathite*,
> or inhab. of Maakah:— Maachathite.
>
> 4603. מָעַל **mâ'al**, *maw-al´*; a prim. root;
> prop. *to cover* up; used only fig. *to act*
> *covertly*, i.e. *treacherously*:— trans-
> gress, (commit, do a) trespass (-ing).
>
> 4604. מַעַל **ma'al**, *mah´-al*; from 4603;
> *treachery*, i.e. *sin*:— falsehood, griev-
> ously, sore, transgression, trespass, ×
> very.

4. You find that this word (4603) means "to *cover* up; to act *covertly*, i.e. *treacherously*." The KJV translators rendered this word as "transgress, (commit, do a) trespass (-ing)." Note that the secondary word, 4604, means "treachery," and it was rendered by the KJV translators as "falsehood, grievously, sore, transgression, trespass." Thus, through a combination of ideas from both the primary root and the secondary word, we learn that the word <u>falsehood</u> in the Job passage derives from "to trespass, creating a grievous and sore situation by uttering a falsehood treacherously, covertly, and with intent to cover up."

3. An Advanced Search: When the Hebrew Word Is from More than One Root

This advanced exercise involves tracing down multiple roots for a Hebrew word. The Hebrew language uses combinations in many proper names. We will walk through finding the meaning of Hebrew names.

Let's assume that you are reading 2 Kings 14:2. You would like to know the Hebrew words from which Jehoaddan, King Amaziah's mother, has been translated. Follow these steps:

1. In the main concordance section of *Strong's*, look up <u>Jehoaddan</u> and find 2 Kings 14:2: "mother's name was *J*. of Jerusalem   2 Kin 14:2   3086."

> **JEHOADAH** *(je-ho'-a-dah)* See Jarah. Son of Ahaz.
> And Ahaz begat *J* 1Chr 8:36   3085
> *J* begat Alemeth, and Azmaveth, and 1Chr 8:36   3085
> **JEHOADDAH** See Jehoadah.
> **JEHOADDAN** *(je-ho-ad'-dan)* Mother of King Amaziah.
> mother's name was *J* of Jerusalem 2Kin 14:2   3086
> mother's name was *J* of Jerusalem 2Chr 25:1   3086
> **JEHOADDIN** See Jehoaddan.
> **JEHOAHAZ** *(je-ho'-a-haz)* See Ahaziah, Joahaz, Shallum.
> 1. *Son of King Jehu.*
> *J* his son reigned in his stead.................. 2Kin 10:35   3059
> son of Ahaziah king of Judah *J*.............. 2Kin 13:1   3059

2. Note that Strong's number for the Hebrew word for <u>Jehoaddan</u> is 3086. Turn to the Hebrew dictionary in your concordance and find the word numbered 3086.

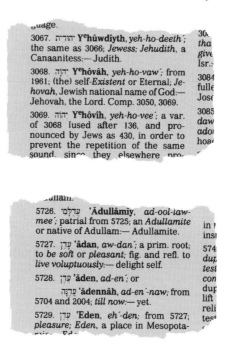

fuller form of 3130; *Jehoseph* ...
Joseph), a son of Jacob:— Joseph.

3085. יְהוֹעַדָּה Yehow'addâh, *yeh-ho-ad-daw*; from 3068 and 5710; *Jehovah-adorned*; *Jehoäddah*, an Isr.:— Je-hoada.

3086. יְהוֹעַדִּין Yehow'addîyn, *yeh-ho-ad-deen*; or

יְהוֹעַדָּן Yehow'addân, *yeh-ho-ad-dawn*; from 3068 and 5727; *Jehovah-pleased*; *Jehoäddin* or *Jehoäddan*, an Israelitess:— Jehoaddan.

3. Note that the Hebrew word for this name, *Yehowaddan,* is derived from two Hebrew words, 3068 and 5727. Turn to both of these words in the Hebrew dictionary:

...guage.

3067. יְהוּדִית Yehûwdîyth, *yeh-ho-deeth*; the same as 3066; *Jewess*; *Jehudith*, a Canaanitess:— Judith.

3068. יְהֹוָה Yehôvâh, *yeh-ho-vaw*; from 1961; (the) self-*Existent* or Eternal; *Je-hovah*, Jewish national name of God:— Jehovah, the Lord. Comp. 3050, 3069.

3069. יְהֹוִה Yehôvih, *yeh-ho-vee*; a var. of 3068 [used after 136, and pro-nounced by Jews as 430, in order to prevent the repetition of the same sound, since they elsewhere pro-

...ullam.

5726. עֲדֻלָּמִי 'Ădullâmîy, *ad-ool-law-mee*; patrial from 5725; an *Adullamite* or native of Adullam:— Adullamite.

5727. עָדַן 'âdan, *aw-dan*; a prim. root; to *be soft* or *pleasant*; fig. and refl. to *live voluptuously*:— delight self.

5728. עֶדֶן 'âden, *ad-en*; or

עֶדֶנָּה 'âdennâh, *ad-en-naw*; from 5704 and 2004; *till now*:— yet.

5729. עֶדֶן 'Eden, *eh-den*; from 5727; *pleasure*; *Eden*, a place in Mesopota-...

4 Notice that word 5727 is a primary word, so our search stops with this word on that track. However, word 3068 is derived from word 1961, so we must turn to that word:

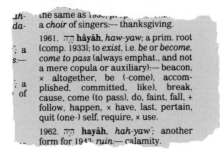

ıh-
da- ıne same as ᴉᵥᵥᵥ, ...
a *choir* of singers:— thanksgiving.

1961. הָיָה **hâyâh,** *haw-yaw;* a prim. root
[comp. 1933]; to *exist,* i.e. *be* or *become,*
come to pass (always emphat., and not
a mere copula or auxiliary):— beacon,
× altogether, be (-come), accom-
plished, committed, like), break,
cause, come (to pass), do, faint, fall, +
follow, happen, × have, last, pertain,
quit (one-) self, require, × use.

1962. הָיָה **hayâh,** *hah-yaw';* another
form for 19⁴³· *ruin:—* calamity.

5. Notice that word 1961 is a primary word, so our search now stops on this track. This diagram shows what we must do now to track down the various meanings of the name *Yehowaddan.*

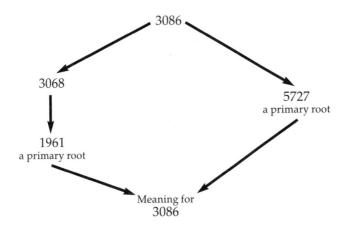

6. Copy down the meanings of word 3068: "self-Existent or Eternal; Jehovah, Jewish national name of God."

7. Copy down the meanings of word 1961: "to exist, be or become."

8. Copy down the meanings of word 5727: "to be soft or pleasant; fig. and refl. to live voluptuously."

9. Now let's combine the two Hebrew words from our diagram to determine a definition for *Yehowaddan*, word 3086:

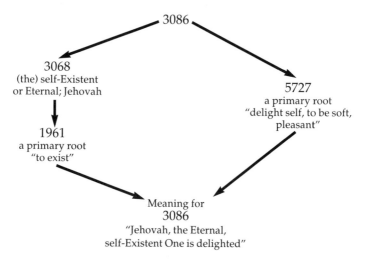

3086

3068
(the) self-Existent
or Eternal; Jehovah

1961
a primary root
"to exist"

5727
a primary root
"delight self, to be soft,
pleasant"

Meaning for
3086
"Jehovah, the Eternal,
self-Existent One is delighted"

10. Thus, Jehoaddan, the mother of King Amaziah, had parents who named her for Yahweh, the Lord. Her name means something like "Yahweh is pleased."

GREEK WORD STUDIES

Doing word studies in the Greek language of the New Testament follows the same procedures as Hebrew word studies. In Greek, you will also be conducting beginning, intermediate, and advanced word studies.

1. A Simple Search: When the Greek Word Is a Primary Root

In this exercise you will learn how to find the Greek root word behind an English word when the underlying Greek word is a primary root.

Imagine that you are reading Titus 2:10, "Not purloining, but shewing all good fidelity, that they may adorn the doctrine of God our Savior in all things." You are interested in the word *purloining*. You want to know the meaning of the Greek behind the English. Follow these steps:

1. In the main concordance section of *Strong's*, look up <u>purloining</u>. You find the Titus 2:10 reference as the only entry under <u>purloining</u>.

```
    ...heir times a
  confirmed these matters of P ................ Est 9:... ö332
PURITY
  in spirit, in faith, in p ........................... 1Ti 4:12      47
  younger as sisters, with all p ................. 1Ti 5:2      47
PURLOINING
  Not p, but shewing all good ................... Titus 2:10   3557
PURPLE
  And blue, and p, and scarlet, and ......... Ex 25:4      713
  fine twined linen, and blue, and p ......... Ex 26:1      713
  shalt make a vail of blue, and p............. Ex 26:31     713
  door of the tent, of blue, and p ............. Ex 26:36     713
  of twenty cubits, of blue, and p ............. Ex 27:16     713
  shall take gold, and blue, and p............. Ex 28:5      713
  ephod of gold, of blue, and of p ........ Ex 2° °    7·
```

2. Note that Strong's number for the Greek word behind <u>purloining</u> is 3557. Turn to the back of your *Strong's Concordance* to the Greek dictionary and find the word numbered 3557.

```
  3502; a brood (or ...........................    2,
  3556. νοσσίον nŏssiŏn, nos-see´-on; di-    tw
  min. of 3502; a birdling:— chicken.       35;
  3557. νοσφίζομαι nŏsphizŏmai, nos-    [51
  fid´-zom-ahee; mid. voice from νοσφί    No
  nŏsphi (apart or clandestinely); to se-    357
  questrate, for oneself, i.e. embezzle:—    dei
  keep back, purloin.                       (fig
  3558. νότος nŏtŏs, not´-os; of uncert.    357
  aff.; the south (-west) wind; by extens.    aff.
  the southern quarter itself:— south
  (wind).
```

3. Here's an explanation of what you see under the word entry 3557.

- The number of the word is followed by the Greek word itself, its English transliteration, and its English pronunciation.

- The information between the English pronunciation and this symbol (:-) is the definition part of the entry. The phrase "mid. voice from *nosphi* (*apart* or *clandestinely*)" means that this word is in the middle form* from *nosphi*, a Greek word which means "apart" or "clandestinely." The further definitions that appear in italics, "to *sequestrate*, for oneself, i.e. *embezzle*," give the various meanings of this word in Greek.

- The different English words that were used by the King James translators to render the meaning of this word in English are listed after the symbol (:-). Note the two words used are "keep back" and "purloin."

- Now that you have discerned the Greek definition of this word, you can take the expanded facets of your English word purloining and have a clearer picture of what it means. Combine the definition part of the entry, "to sequestrate for oneself, i.e. embezzle," with the translation part of the entry, "keep back, purloin." Thus, purloining means "to set apart clandestinely for one's self, to keep back [for one's self], to embezzle."

* According to Vines: "Whereas in English there are only two voices, active and passive, the Greek language has three. The Middle Voice signifies that a person has a special interest in the effects of his action, that he is acting either upon, or for, himself, or that when he is acting for others he has a personal interest in their condition or welfare."

2. An Intermediate Search: When the Greek Word Is from Another Root

In this exercise you will learn how to find the Greek root word behind an English word when the underlying Greek word is from another Greek root.

Let's assume that you are reading John 19:40, "Then took they the body of Jesus, and wound it in linen clothes with the spices, as the manner of the Jews is to bury." You are interested in the word *manner*. You want to know the meaning of the Greek behind this English word. Follow these steps:

1. In the main concordance section of *Strong's*, look up manner. You find the John 19:40 entry: "as the *m* of the Jews is to bury Jn 19:40   1485."

What *m* of communications are	Lk 24:17	
after the *m* of the purifying of	Jn 2:6	
What *m* of saying is this that he	Jn 7:36	
as the *m* of the Jews is to bury	Jn 19:40	1485
shall so come in like *m* as ye	Acts 1:11	5158
Wherein were all *m* of fourfooted	Acts 10:12	1485
circumcised after the *m* of Moses	Acts 15:1	1485

2. Note that Strong's number for the Greek word behind <u>manner</u> is 1485. Turn to the back of your *Strong's Concordance* to the Greek dictionary and find the word numbered 1485.

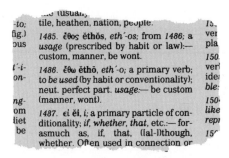

> 1484. ἔθνος εthnos, ..., c.
> from *1486*; a *race* (as of the same *habit*),
> i.e. a *tribe*; spec. a *foreign* (non-Jewish) 15ι
> one (usually by impl. *pagan*):— Gen- aff.
> tile, heathen, nation, people. 150
>
> 1485. ἔθος ēthŏs, *eth´-os*; from *1486*; a ver
> *usage* (prescribed by habit or law):— pla
> custom, manner, be wont. 150
>
> 1486. ἔθω ēthō, *eth´-o*; a primary verb; ver
> to *be used* (by habit or conventionality); ide
> neut. perfect part. *usage*:— be custom ble
> (manner, wont). 1ᵉ

3. Note that all the elements of this entry are the same as they were for the simple search for a Greek primary word which you have just completed—with this exception: Word number 1485, meaning "a usage (prescribed by habit or law)," is not a primary root, but it derives from word 1486, which is the primary root. Turn to this word.

> ...e (usuaιι
> -to; tile, heathen, nation, peυριe. 1ᵟ.
> fig.) 1485. ἔθος ēthŏs, *eth´-os*; from *1486*; a ver
> ους *usage* (prescribed by habit or law):— pla
> custom, manner, be wont. 150.
>
> t´-i- 1486. ἔθω ēthō, *eth´-o*; a primary verb; ver
> on- to *be used* (by habit or conventionality); ide
> neut. perfect part. *usage*:— be custom ble
> ng- (manner, wont). 150ᴇ
> om 1487. εἰ ĕi, *i*; a primary particle of con- like
> liet ditionality; *if, whether, that*, etc.:— for- repι
> be asmuch as, if, that, ((al-))though, 15ᵞ
> whether. Often used in connection or

4. You find that this word (1486) means "to *be used* (by habit or conventionality)." The KJV translators rendered this word as "by custom, manner, wont." Thus, by combining the ideas from both the primary root and the secondary word, we learn that the word <u>manner</u> in John 19:40 shows that it was the custom of the Jews—their manner, their habit—to bury their dead in a particular way (with spices and the body wrapped in linen).

3. An Advanced Search: When the Greek Word Is from More than One Root

This advanced exercise involves tracing down multiple roots for a Greek word. This search is conducted just like the advanced Hebrew exercise that you have already conducted.

Suppose you are reading John 3:16. The word *begotten* strikes your interest. You want to know the meaning of the Greek word from which this English word has been translated. Follow these steps:

1. In the main concordance section of *Strong's,* look up <u>begotten</u> and find John 3:16: "that he gave his only *b* Son   Jn 3:16 3439."

```
  ... ...er unto you ...
  these are the b of sorrows ....................... MK 13:8        ...6
BEGOTTEN
  b Seth were eight hundred years ........... Gen 5:4        3205
  b of thy father, she is thy ..................... Lev 18:11      4138
  have I b them, that thou ........................ Num 11:12     3205
  The children that are b of them ............. Deut 23:8      3205
  and ten sons of his body b ..................... Judg 8:30     3318
  or who hath b the drops of dew ............. Job 38:28      3205
  this day have I b thee ............................ Ps 2:7          3205
  thine heart, Who hath b me these ........... Is 49:21       3205
  for they have b strange children ............. Hos 5:7        3205
  as of the only b of the Father ................. Jn 1:14        3439
  the only b Son, which is in the .............. Jn 1:18        3439
  that he gave his only b Son .................... Jn 3:16        3439
  the name of the only b Son of God........ Jn 3:18        3439
  my Son, this day have I b thee .............. Acts 13:33     1080
```

2. Note that Strong's number for the Greek word behind <u>begotten</u> is 3439. Turn to the back of your concordance to the Greek dictionary and find the word numbered 3439.

```
  quarrel.                                            ...
  3438. μονή mŏnē, mon-ay'; from 3306; a      34;
  staying, i.e. residence (the act or the       34;
  place):— abode, mansion.
                                                 34t
  3439. μονογενής mŏnŏgĕnēs, mon-og-   de;
  en-ace'; from 3441 and 1096; only-born,    My
  i.e. sole:— only (begotten, child).
                                                 34t
  3440. μόνον mŏnŏn, mon'-on; neut. of  34t
  3441 as adv.; merely:— alone, but, only.    'm;
  3441. μόνος mŏnŏs, mon'-os; prob.      sar
  from 3306; remaining, i.e. sole or single;  3.
  by impl. mere:— alone, only, by them-
```

3. Note that this one Greek word (3439) is derived from two Greek words: 3441 and 1096.

en-ace'; from ... ...
i.e. *sole:*— only (begotten, child).

3440. μόνον **mŏnŏn**, *mon'-on*; neut. of
3441 as adv.; *merely:*— alone, but, only.

3441. μόνος **mŏnŏs**, *mon'-os*; prob.
from **3306**; *remaining*, i.e. *sole* or *single*;
by impl. *mere:*— alone, only, by themselves.

3442. μονόφθαλμος **mŏnŏphthalmŏs**,
mon-of'-thal-mos; from **3441** and **3788**;
one-eyed:— with one eye.

3443. μονόω **mŏnŏō**, *mon-ŏ'-o*; from

old.

1096. γίνομαι **ginŏmai**, *ghin'-om-ahee*;
a prol. and mid. voice form of a primary verb; to *cause to be* ("*gen*"-*erate*),
i.e. (refl.) to *become* (*come into being*),
used with great latitude (lit., fig., intens., etc.):— arise, be assembled, be
(-come, -fall, -have self), be brought (to
pass), (be) come (to pass), continue, be
divided, draw, be ended, fall, be fin-
ished, follow, be found, be fulfilled, +
God forbid, grow, happen, have, be
kept, be made, be married, be ordained to be, partake, pass, be per-
formed, be published, require, seem,
be showed, × soon as it was, sound, be
taken, be turned, use, wax, will, would,
be wrought.

1097. γινώσκω **ginōskō**, *ghin-oce'-ko*; a
prol. form of a primary verb; to "*know*"
(absolutely) in a great variety of appli-

4. Note that word 1096 is a primary word, so our search stops with this word on that track. However, word 3441 is derived from word 3306, so we must turn to that word:

3303 and 5104, ...
ever:— also, but, howbeit, neverthe-
less, yet.

3306. μένω **mĕnō**, *men'-o*; a primary
verb; to *stay* (in a given place, state,
relation or expectancy):— abide, continue, dwell, endure, be present, remain, stand, tarry (for), × thine own.

3307. μερίζω **mĕrizō**, *mer-id'-zo*; from
3313; to *part*, i.e. (lit.) to *apportion*, be-
stow, *share*, or (fig.) to *disunite*, *dif-
fer:*— deal, be difference between, dis-
tribute, divide, give part.

5. Notice that word 3306 is a primary word, so our search now stops on this track. This diagram shows what we must do now to track down the various meanings of the Greek word behind the English word <u>begotten</u>:

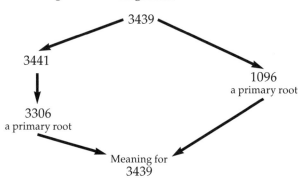

6. Copy down the meanings of words 3441, 3306, and 1096. Here's how all this information looks when entered on the diagram above:

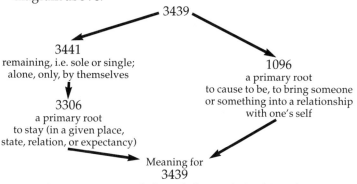

7. Thus, the Greek word for <u>begotten</u> in John 3:16 can be understood as "God bringing someone into a special and permanent relationship with Himself." Jesus, the Son of God, occupies a single, unique, one-of-a-kind, permanent relationship with God. <u>Begotten</u> does not mean that God gave birth to Jesus. Jesus was the exact image of God and thus was equal to the invisible God. Jesus has always been in the unique position of being the Son of God. He chose to be the One whom God would send to be the sacrifice for the world. No one else in the universe occupies this place.

Using *Strong's* for Expanded Word Studies

Many times in your Bible reading you come across a biblical word and you want to know the underlying definition. In Chapter 3, by using the dictionaries provided in the back of *Strong's Concordance,* we found a simple definition. By combining Strong's definition of a word and the various ways the word is translated by the King James Version, we derived a simple composite definition.

There are times, however, when you may want to examine the fuller picture a word can paint for you. In this chapter we will repeat some of what you have learned previously. But this time we will be doing more advanced word studies.

STUDYING WHERE A WORD OCCURS ELSEWHERE IN THE BIBLE

In this exercise you will learn how to find a Greek or Hebrew word behind an English word and then study where that particular word occurs elsewhere in the Bible. By now you can easily find the original word behind an English word. But if you view a word in other contexts, you can draw additional insights about the word. For a model of a simple word study, let's take an example from the Greek New Testament. The steps in this exercise apply equally to a study done in the Old Testament.

Let's assume that you are reading Matthew 23:23: "Woe unto you, scribes and Pharisees, hypocrites! for ye pay tithe of mint and anise and cummin, and have omitted the weightier matters of the law, judgment, mercy, and faith: these ought ye to have done, and not to leave the other undone." You want to know what the word *tithe* means in this passage as well as other places in the Bible. Follow these steps:

1. Look up the word <u>tithe</u> in the main concordance section of *Strong's* and trace down the column to find Matthew 23:23.

> ...the LORD said to ....
> And he said, It is Elijah the *T* 2Kin 1:8   8664
> spake by his servant Elijah the *T* 2Kin 9:36   8664
>
> **TITHE**
>   all the *t* of the land, whether of .... Lev 27:30   4643
>   And concerning the *t* of the herd .... Lev 27:32   4643
>   LORD, even a tenth part of the *t* .... Num 18:26   4643
>   thy gates the *t* of thy corn .... Deut 12:17   4643
>   Thou shalt truly *t* all the .... Deut 14:22   6237
>   the *t* of thy corn, of thy wine, ... Deut 14:23   4643
>   thou shalt bring forth all the *t* .... Deut 14:28   4643
>   the *t* of all things brought they 2Chr 31:5   4643
>   also brought in the *t* of oxen 2Chr 31:6   4643
>   the *t* of holy things which were 2Chr 31:6   4643
>   the Levites shall bring up the *t* .... Neh 10:38   4643
>   all Judah the *t* of the corn .... Neh 13:12   4643
>   **for ye pay *t* of mint and anise and** .... Mt 23:23   *586*
>   **for ye *t* mint and rue and all** .... Lk 11:42   *586*
>
> **TITHES**
>   And he gave him *t* of all .... Gen 14:20   4643
>   will at all redeem ought of his *t* .... Lev 27:31   4643
>   But the *t* of the children of .... Num 18:24   4643

2. Note that the Greek word behind <u>tithe</u> in this passage is word 586. Turn to the Greek dictionary in *Strong's* and find the word numbered 586.

> 585. ἀπόδειξις **apodeixis**, *ap-od´-ixe-sis;* from *584; manifestation:*— demonstration.
>
> 586. ἀποδεκατόω **apŏdĕkatŏō**, *ap-od-ek-at-ŏ´-o;* from *575* and *1183;* to *tithe* (as debtor or creditor):— (give, pay, take) tithe.
>
> 587. ἀπόδεκτος **apŏdĕktŏs**, *ap-od´-ek-tos;* from *588; accepted,* i.e. *agreeable:*— acceptable.

3. You will see that word 586 comes from two Greek root words, 575 and 1183. Turn to these words:

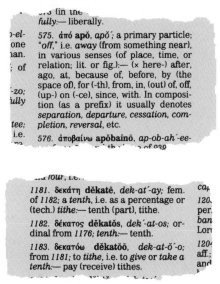

> ..s (in the
> *fully.*— liberally.
>
>)-el-   575. ἀπό **apŏ**, *apŏ´*; a primary particle;
> one   *"off,"* i.e. *away* (from something near),
> ian.   in various senses (of place, time, or
> ; of   relation; lit. or fig.):— (× here-) after,
>   ago, at, because of, before, by (the
>   space of), for (-th), from, in, (out) of, off,
> -zo;   (up-) on (-ce), since, with. In composi-
> ully   tion (as a prefix) it usually denotes
>   *separation, departure, cessation, com-*
> tee;   *pletion, reversal,* etc.
> i.e.   576. ἀποβαίνω **apŏbainō**, *ap-ob-ah´-ee-*

> ..u *four*, ι.e..
>
> 1181. δεκάτη **dĕkatē**, *dek-at´-ay*; fem.   *ca*,
> of *1182*; a *tenth*, i.e. as a percentage or   120,
> (tech.) *tithe:*— tenth (part), tithe.   per,
> 1182. δέκατος **dĕkatŏs**, *dek´-at-os*; or-   *ban*
> dinal from *1176*; *tenth:*— tenth.   Lor
> 1183. δεκατόω **dĕkatŏō**, *dek-at-ŏ´-o*;   120,
> from *1181*; to *tithe*, i.e. to *give* or *take a*   aff.;
> *tenth:*— pay (receive) tithes.   and

4. Draw a diagram of these words as you have done in previous exercises, showing the root word and two secondary words that feed into the meaning of this Greek word:

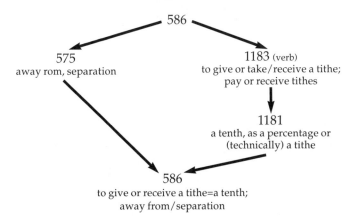

586

575
away rom, separation

1183 (verb)
to give or take/receive a tithe;
pay or receive tithes

1181
a tenth, as a percentage or
(technically) a tithe

586
to give or receive a tithe=a tenth;
away from/separation

5. You conclude that a tithe is a tenth of something; it is given and/or received; it is totally away from/separated from the giver (no longer his to determine its use; no strings remain attached to a tithe).

6. After deriving this definition, return to the word <u>tithe</u> in the main concordance section of *Strong's*. Scan the columns for other forms of word 586. You find <u>tithes</u> and <u>tithing</u>.

TIPHSAH	1369	TOBIJAH

<table>
<tr><td>put it upon the t of the right</td><td>Lev 14:25</td><td>8571</td></tr>
<tr><td>that is in his hand upon the t of</td><td>Lev 14:28</td><td>8571</td></tr>
<tr><td>that he may dip the t of his</td><td>Lk 16:24</td><td>206</td></tr>
</table>

TIPHSAH *(tif·sah)*
1. A city on the Euphrates River.
from *T* even to Azzah, over all ...... 1Kin 4:24 — 8607
2. A city in Judah.
Then Menahem smote *T*, and all that ... 2Kin 15:16 — 8607

TIRAS *(Ti·ras)* *A son of Japheth.*
Javan, and Tubal, and Meshech, and *T* .. Gen 10:2 — 8493
Javan, and Tubal, and Meshech, and *T* .. 1Chr 1:5 — 8493

TIRATHITES *(ti·rath·ites)* *A family of scribes.*
the *T*, the Shimeathites, and .... 1Chr 2:55 — 8654

TIRE
bind the *t* of thine head upon .... Eze 24:17 — 6287

TIRED
t her head, and looked out at a .... 2Kin 9:30 — 3190

TIRES
their round *t* like the moon, ... Is 3:18 — 7720
your *t* shall be upon your heads, ... Eze 24:23 — 6287

TIRHAKAH *(tur·ha'·kah)* *A king of Ethiopia.*
heard say of *T* king of Ethiopia .... 2Kin 19:9 — 8640
say concerning *T* king of Ethiopia .... Is 37:9 — 8640

TIRHANAH *(tur·ha'·nah)* *A son of Caleb.*
concubine, bare Sheber, and *T* .... 1Chr 2:48 — 8647

TIRIA *(tir·e·ah)* *A descendant of Judah.*
Ziph, and Ziphah, *T*, and Asareel....... 1Chr 4:16 — 8493

TIRSHATHA *(tur·sha·thah)* *Persian governors of Judah.*
the *T* said unto them, that they........... Ezr 2:63 — 8660
the *T* said unto them, that they........... Neh 7:65 — 8660
The *T* gave to the treasure a............. Neh 7:70 — 8660
And Nehemiah, which is the *T*........... Neh 8:9 — 8660
that sealed were, Nehemiah, the *T*........ Neh 10:1 — 8660

TIRZAH *(tur'·zah)*
1. A daughter of Zelophehad.
and Noah, Hoglah, Milcah, and *T* .... Num 26:33 — 8656
Noah, and Hoglah, and Milcah, and *T*... Num 27:1 — 8656
For Mahlah, *T*, and Hoglah, and .... Num 36:11 — 8656
and Noah, Hoglah, Milcah, and *T* .... Josh 17:3 — 8656
2. A city in Ephraim.
The king of *T*, one .... Josh 12:24 — 8656
arose, and departed, and came to *T* ..... 1Kin 14:17 — 8656
building of Ramah, and dwelt in *T* ...... 1Kin 15:21 — 8656
to reign over all Israel in *T* .... 1Kin 15:33 — 8656
his fathers, and was buried in *T* .... 1Kin 16:6 — 8656
Baasha to reign over Israel in *T* .... 1Kin 16:8 — 8656
against him, as he was in *T* .... 1Kin 16:9 — 8656
of Arza steward of his house in *T* .... 1Kin 16:9 — 8656
did Zimri reign seven days in *T* .... 1Kin 16:15 — 8656
with him, and they besieged *T*........... 1Kin 16:17 — 8656
six years reigned he in *T* .... 1Kin 16:23 — 8656
the son of Gadi went up from *T* .... 2Kin 15:14 — 8656
and the coasts thereof from *T* .... 2Kin 15:16 — 8656
art beautiful, O my love, as *T* .... Song 6:4 — 8656

TISHBE See TISHBITE.

TISHBITE *(tish'·bite)* *An inhabitant of Tishbeh.*
And Elijah the *T*, who was of the .... 1Kin 17:1 — 8664
of the LORD came to Elijah the *T* .... 1Kin 21:17 — 8664
of the LORD came to Elijah the *T* .... 1Kin 21:28 — 8664
of the LORD said to Elijah the *T* .... 2Kin 1:3 — 8664
And he said, It is Elijah the *T*........... 2Kin 1:8 — 8664
spake by his servant Elijah the *T* .... 2Kin 9:36 — 8664

TITHE
all the *t* of the land, whether of .... Lev 27:30 — 4643
And concerning the *t* of the herd .... Lev 27:32 — 4643
LORD, even a tenth part of the *t* .... Num 18:26 — 4643
thy gates the *t* of thy corn .... Deut 12:17 — 4643
Thou shalt truly *t* all the .... Deut 14:22 — 6237
the *t* of thy corn, of thy wine, ... Deut 14:23 — 4643
thou shalt bring forth all the *t* .... Deut 14:28 — 4643
the *t* of all thought they .... 2Chr 31:6 — 4643
also brought in the *t* of oxen .... 2Chr 31:6 — 4643
the *t* of holy things were .... 2Chr 31:6 — 4643
the Levites shall bring up the *t* .... Neh 10:38 — 4643
all Judah the *t* of the corn .... Neh 13:12 — 4643
for ye pay *t* of mint and anise and.... Mt 23:23 — 586
for ye *t* mint and rue and all .... Lk 11:42 — 586

TITHES
And he gave him *t* of all .... Gen 14:20 — 4643
will at all redeem ought of his *t*........ Lev 27:31 — 4643
But the *t* of the children of .... Num 18:24 — 4643
the *t* which I have given you from ...... Num 18:26 — 4643
unto the LORD all your *t*................ Num 18:28 — 4643

<table>
<tr><td>and your sacrifices, and your t</td><td>Deut 12:6</td><td>4643</td></tr>
<tr><td>and your sacrifices, your t</td><td>Deut 12:11</td><td>4643</td></tr>
<tr><td>the t of thine increase the third</td><td>Deut 26:12</td><td>4643</td></tr>
<tr><td>brought in the offerings and the t</td><td>2Chr 31:12</td><td>4643</td></tr>
<tr><td>the t of our ground unto the</td><td>Neh 10:37</td><td>4643</td></tr>
<tr><td>the t in all the cities of our</td><td>Neh 10:37</td><td>6237</td></tr>
<tr><td>Levites, when the Levites take t</td><td>Neh 10:38</td><td>6237</td></tr>
<tr><td>the t unto the house of our God</td><td>Neh 10:38</td><td>4643</td></tr>
<tr><td>for the firstfruits, and for the t</td><td>Neh 12:44</td><td>4643</td></tr>
<tr><td>the t of the corn, the new wine,</td><td>Neh 13:5</td><td>4643</td></tr>
<tr><td>and your t after three years</td><td>Amos 4:4</td><td>4643</td></tr>
<tr><td>In t and offerings</td><td>Mal 3:8</td><td>4643</td></tr>
<tr><td>Bring ye all the t into the</td><td>Mal 3:10</td><td>4643</td></tr>
<tr><td>I give t of all that I possess</td><td>Lk 18:12</td><td>586</td></tr>
<tr><td>have a commandment to take t of</td><td>Heb 7:5</td><td>586</td></tr>
<tr><td>from them received t of Abraham</td><td>Heb 7:6</td><td>1183</td></tr>
<tr><td>And here men that die receive t</td><td>Heb 7:8</td><td>1181</td></tr>
<tr><td>say, Levi also, who receiveth t</td><td>Heb 7:9</td><td>1183</td></tr>
<tr><td>payed t in Abraham</td><td>Heb 7:9</td><td>1183</td></tr>
</table>

TITHING
end of *t* all the tithes of thine .... Deut 26:12 — 6237
year, which is the year of *t* .... Deut 26:12 — 4643

TITUS See JUSTUS.

TITUS JUSTUS See JUSTUS.

TITLE
What *t* is that that I see .... 2Kin 23:17 — 6725
And Pilate wrote a *t*, and put it on ..... Jn 19:19 — 5102
This *t* then read many of the Jews ...... Jn 19:20 — 5102

TITLES
let me give flattering *t* unto man .... Job 32:21 — —
I know not to give flattering *t* .... Job 32:22 — —

TITTLE
one jot or one *t* shall in no wise .... Mt 5:18 — 2762
than one *t* of the law to fail .... Lk 16:17 — 2762

TITUS *(ti'·tus)* *A co-worker with Paul.*
because I found not *T* my brother ...... 2Cor 2:13 — 5103
comforted by the coming of *T* .... 2Cor 7:6 — 5103
more joyed we for the joy of *T* .... 2Cor 7:13 — 5103
boasting, which I made before *T* .... 2Cor 7:14 — 5103
Insomuch that we desired *T* .... 2Cor 8:6 — 5103
care into the heart of *T* for you .... 2Cor 8:16 — 5103
Whether any do enquire of *T* .... 2Cor 8:23 — 5103
I desired *T*, and with him I sent a ...... 2Cor 12:18 — 5103
Did *T* make a gain of you .... 2Cor 12:18 — 5103
a city of Macedonia, by *T* .... 2Cor s — 5103
Barnabas, and took *T* with me also .... Gal 2:1 — 5103
But neither *T*, who was with me,....... Gal 2:3 — 5103
to Galatia, *T* unto Dalmatia............ 2Ti 4:10 — 5103
To *T*, mine own son after the .... Titus 1:4 — 5103
It was written to *T*, ordained the .... Titus s — 5103

TIZITE *(ti'·zite)* *Family name of Joha.*
and Joha his brother, the *T*.............. 1Chr 11:45 — 8491

TO See APPENDIX.

TOAH *(to'·ah)* See NAHATH, TOHU. *An ancestor of Samuel.*
the son of Eliel, the son of *T* .... 1Chr 6:34 — 8430

TOB *(tob)* *A district in Syria.*
and dwelt in the land of *T*.............. Judg 11:3 — 2897
Jephthah out of the land of *T* .... Judg 11:5 — 2897

TOB-ADONIJAH *(tob'·ad·o·ni·jah)* *A Levite messenger of King Jehoshaphat.*
and Adonijah, and Tobijah, and *T*...... 2Chr 17:8 — 2899

TOBIAH *(to·bi'·ah)* See TOBIJAH.
1. A family of exiles.
of Delaiah, the children of *T*............ Ezr 2:60 — 2900
of Delaiah, the children of *T*............ Neh 7:62 — 2900
2. An Ammonite who opposed Nehemiah.
T the servant, the Ammonite, ... Neh 2:10 — 2900
T the servant, the Ammonite, and ...... Neh 2:19 — 2900
Now *T* the Ammonite was by him, and .. Neh 4:3 — 2900
pass, that when Sanballat, and *T*....... Neh 4:7 — 2900
to pass, when Sanballat, and *T* .... Neh 6:1 — 2900
for *T* and Sanballat had hired him...... Neh 6:12 — 2900
My God, think thou upon *T* .... Neh 6:14 — 2900
of Judah sent many letters unto *T* ..... Neh 6:17 — 2900
the letters of *T* came unto them .... Neh 6:17 — 2900
T sent letters to put me in fear .... Neh 6:19 — 2900
of our God, was allied unto *T* .... Neh 13:4 — 2900
the evil that Eliashib did for *T*.......... Neh 13:7 — 2900
stuff of *T* out of the chamber........... Neh 13:8 — 2900

TOBIJAH *(to·bi'·jah)* See TOBIAH.
1. A Levite messenger of King Jehoshaphat.
and Jehonathan, and Adonijah, and *T* .. 2Chr 17:8 — 2900

T

7. Look for verses under <u>tithe</u>, <u>tithes</u>, and <u>tithing</u> that use the same Greek word, 586, which you are researching. You find four verses that use this Greek word:

- "Woe unto you, scribes and Pharisees, hypocrites! for ye pay tithe of mint and anise and cummin, and have omitted the weightier matters of the law, judgment, mercy, and faith: these ought ye to have done, and not to leave the other undone" (Matt. 23:23).

- "But woe unto you, Pharisees! for ye tithe mint and rue and all manner of herbs, and pass over judgment and the love of God: these ought ye to have done, and not to leave the other undone" (Luke 11:42).

- "I [a Pharisee speaking] fast twice in the week, I give tithes of all that I possess" (Luke 18:12).

- "And verily they that are of the sons of Levi, who receive the office of the priesthood, have a commandment to take tithes of the people according to the law, that is, of their brethren, though they come out of the loins of Abraham" (Heb. 7:5).

8. Analyze how your definition of <u>tithe</u> fits in each of these instances. Then make some observations concerning tithing from the context of these four verses.

- Who tithes? Scribes, Pharisees, hypocrites, people, brethren of the sons of Levi.

- What is tithed? Mint, anise, cummin, all herbs, rue, all possessions not specified.

- Where are tithes paid and collected? This is not specified in these four verses.

- When are tithes paid and collected? This is not specified in these four verses.

- Why are tithes paid and collected? This is not specified in these four verses.

- Other pertinent information: Jesus said that the Pharisees "ought to have tithed." The sons of Levi were commanded to receive tithes.

9. From just these four New Testament uses of the word tithe (Greek word 586) we can learn a lot. Tithes are a tenth (by definition) and were collected. The lone Pharisee tithed all of his possessions. The Pharisees were tithing even their herbs [we might say salt, pepper, and cinnamon]. The Pharisees were meticulous in tithing even the grains of their herbs; yet they neglected mercy, faith, and the love of God. Jesus condemned them for their neglect. However, he admonished them not to forsake the tithe.

The above are safe observations that can be made from these four uses of Greek word 586. But we have considered only four verses from the New Testament. No verses from the Old Testament have been studied. Therefore, this study is incomplete.

Many people will use just a verse or two from the Bible and derive a doctrine from these verses. A doctrine is what the Bible teaches on a particular subject. In order to produce a biblical doctrine, the study needs to be exhaustive. To complete this study, you will need to study all the verses on tithing in the Old Testament. Look up, observe, record, and summarize how the word *tithe* is used in the Old Testament by following the steps above. Then combine your studies from both testaments into a complete word study on the English word *tithe*.

COMPARING A WORD WITH ITS OTHER BACKGROUND WORDS

In this exercise you will learn how to find the Greek or Hebrew word behind an English word and then compare this word with its other background words throughout the Bible—Old Testament and New Testament.

Let's assume that you are doing a study in Exodus 16:7 on the word *murmur.* You would like to do an extensive study of the Hebrew word behind this English word. Here are the steps to follow:

1. Draw a line across the middle of a sheet of paper, labeling the top "Old Testament" and the bottom half "New Testament."

2. In the main concordance section of *Strong's* look up the word murmur.

```
..., m, drunk...
Neither repented they of their m ............ Rev 9:21    5408
```

MURMUR
what are we, that ye *m* against us	Ex 16:7	3885
murmurings which ye *m* against him	Ex 16:8	3885
congregation, which *m* against me	Num 14:27	3885
Israel, which they *m* against me	Num 14:27	3885
the congregation to *m* against him	Num 14:36	3885
is Aaron, that ye *m* against him...........	Num 16:11	3885
whereby they *m* against you	Num 17:5	3885
unto them, *M* not among yourselves......	Jn 6:43	*1111*
Neither *m* ye, as some of them	1Cor 10:10	*1111*

MURMURED
the people *m* against Moses, ...	Ex 15:24	3885
of Israel *m* against Moses...........	Ex 16:2	388-

3. Scan down the word <u>murmur</u> and its derivatives (<u>murmured</u>, <u>murmurers</u>, <u>murmuring</u>, <u>murmurings</u>).

MURDERERS
the children of the *m* he slew not...........	2Kin 14:6	5221
lodged in it; but now *m*.....................	Is 1:21	7523
my soul is wearied because of *m*..........	Jer 4:31	2026
his armies, and destroyed those *m*........	Mt 22:7	5406
have been now the betrayers and *m*.......	Acts 7:52	5406
four thousand men that were *m*............	Acts 21:38	4607
for *m* of fathers and *m* of.................	1Ti 1:9	3964
m of mothers, for manslayers,..............	1Ti 1:9	3389
and the abominable, and *m*, and...........	Rev 21:8	5406
sorcerers, and whoremongers, and *m* ...	Rev 22:15	5406

MURDERS
heart proceed evil thoughts, *m*	Mt 15:19	5408
adulteries, fornications, *m*................	Mk 7:21	5408
Envyings, *m*, drunkenness, ...	Gal 5:21	5408
Neither repented they of their *m*	Rev 9:21	5408

MURMUR
what are we, that ye *m* against us	Ex 16:7	3885
murmurings which ye *m* against him	Ex 16:8	3885
congregation, which *m* against me	Num 14:27	3885
Israel, which they *m* against me	Num 14:27	3885
the congregation to *m* against him	Num 14:36	3885
is Aaron, that ye *m* against him...........	Num 16:11	3885
whereby they *m* against you	Num 17:5	3885
unto them, *M* not among yourselves	Jn 6:43	*1111*
Neither *m* ye, as some of them	1Cor 10:10	*1111*

MURMURED
the people *m* against Moses, ...	Ex 15:24	3885
of Israel *m* against Moses....................	Ex 16:2	3885
the people *m* against Moses, and	Ex 17:3	3885

of Israel *m* against Moses......................	Num 14:2	3885
upward, which have *m* against me........	Num 14:29	3885
of Israel *m* against Moses....................	Num 16:41	3885
ye *m* in your tents, and said,................	Deut 1:27	7279
m against the princes.........................	Josh 9:18	3885
But in that day *m* against me...............	Ps 106:25	7279
they that *m* shall learn doctrine	Is 29:24	7279
they *m* against the goodman of the	Mt 20:11	*1111*
And they *m* against her.......................	Mk 14:5	*1690*
Pharisees *m* against his disciples	Lk 5:30	*1111*
And the Pharisees and scribes *m*	Lk 15:2	*1234*
And when they saw it, they all *m*	Lk 19:7	*1234*
The Jews then *m* at him, because........	Jn 6:41	*1111*
that his disciples *m* at it.....................	Jn 6:61	*1111*
m such things concerning him..............	Jn 7:32	*1111*
murmur ye, as some of them also *m*	1Cor 10:10	*1111*

MURMURERS
These are *m*, complainers, walking	Jude 16	*1113*

MURMURING
there was much *m* among the people	Jn 7:12	*1112*
there arose a *m* of the Grecians	Acts 6:1	*1112*

MURMURINGS
heareth your *m* against the LORD..........	Ex 16:7	8519
m which ye murmur against him	Ex 16:8	8519
your *m* are not against us, but..............	Ex 16:8	8519
for he hath heard your *m*....................	Ex 16:9	8519
I have heard the *m* of the	Ex 16:12	8519
I have heard the *m* of the....................	Num 14:27	8519
the *m* of the children of Israel..............	Num 17:5	8519
quite take away their *m* from me..........	Num 17:10	8519
Do all things without *m* and	Phil 2:14	*1112*

4. As you scan down the various derivatives, note the different Hebrews words for this concept used in the Old Testament. Record these Hebrew words on the Old Testament section of your study sheet: 3885, 7279, and 8519. Then record the Greek words on the New Testament section of your study sheet: 1111, 1690, 1234, 1113, and 1112.

This means there are three different Hebrew words translated into the one English word <u>murmur</u>. You will notice five different Greek words [or their roots] are translated into this one English word. Observing that a few of the numbers are close may hint that these are derivatives of one Greek word [e.g., 1111, 1112, 1113].

5. Look up each of these words in the Hebrew and Greek dictionaries in *Strong's Concordance*. Note whether they are root words or secondary words, using the knowledge you have gained from previous exercises in this book. Record the definitions of these words under the appropriate sections of your study sheet. Your chart should look like this after you have researched all the words for <u>murmur</u>:

Old Testament

3885: To stop, stay, spend the night, complain [to stay focused on one event].

7279: To grumble, rebel.

8519: From 3885, obstinacy.

New Testament

1111: To grumble, murmur.

1112: From 1111, a grumbling, grudging, murmuring.

1113: From 1111, a grumbler, murmurer.

1234: From 1233 (through) and 1111, to complain throughout a crowd, murmur.

1690: To murmur against.

6. By carefully and diligently recording all of your observations, you will be able to conclude that a person who murmurs focuses on one situation to the exclusion of everything else. The dissatisfaction felt is not shouted but voiced quietly throughout a group. You might say such a person "camps" or "parks" on a point for a time of discussion. Obstinacy means to stand against. Murmuring is an infectious disease that causes dissension, lack of trust in leadership, and rebellion against God's chosen leaders.

TRACING A WORD AND ITS SYNONYMS THROUGHOUT THE BIBLE

This advanced study is a culmination of all the previous studies you have done. You will begin with a simple definition study, progress through an intermediate study, and then conclude with a cycle of studies on synonyms. Let's use the word *joy* as an example for this advanced word study. Follow these steps:

1. Draw a line across the middle of a study sheet, labeling the top half "Old Testament" and the bottom half "New Testament."

2. Look up joy in the main concordance section of *Strong's*.

3. As you scan down the joy entry, note all the different Hebrew words translated as "joy" in the Old Testament. Record these entry words and their roots and definitions on the Old Testament section of your study sheet. (Below is the study sheet with all these conclusions listed. The words in brackets are other English translations of this *Strong's* entry. These would need to be pursued to complete an exhaustive study on joy.)

Old Testament

1523: To spin around (under the influence of emotion).

1524: From 1523, a revolution.

1525: From 1524, joy, rejoicing.

2305: To rejoice [make glad, be joined (hand in hand dancing for joy)].

2416: From 2421, alive, fresh, strong [many other words].

2896: From 2895, to do or make good [cheer, please, etc.].

2898: From 2895, good [fair, go well with, etc.].

4885: From 7797, delight [joy, mirth].

5937: To jump for joy, exult [triumph].

5947: From 5937, exultant.

JOY

king Saul, with tabrets, with *j*	1Sa 18:6	8057
pipes, and rejoiced with great *j*	1Kin 1:40	8057
for there was *j* in Israel	1Chr 12:40	8057
by lifting up the voice with *j*	1Chr 15:16	8057
of the house of Obed-edom with *j*	1Chr 15:25	8057
king also rejoiced with great *j*	1Chr 29:9	8057
now have I seen with *j* thy people	1Chr 29:17	8057
to go again to Jerusalem with *j*	2Chr 20:27	8057
So there was great *j* in Jerusalem	2Chr 30:26	8057
and many shouted aloud for *j*	Ezr 3:12	8057
the noise of the shout of *j* from	Ezr 3:13	8057
of this house of God with *j*	Ezr 6:16	2305
bread seven days with *j*	Ezr 6:22	8057
for the *j* of the LORD is your	Neh 8:10	2304
made them rejoice with great *j*	Neh 12:43	8057
so that the *j* of Jerusalem was	Neh 12:43	8057
Jews had light, and gladness, and *j*	Est 8:16	8342
his decree came, the Jews had *j*	Est 8:17	8057
turned unto them from sorrow to *j*	Est 9:22	8057
make them days of feasting and *j*	Est 9:22	8057
Behold, this is the *j* of his way	Job 8:19	4885
the *j* of the hypocrite but for a	Job 20:5	8057
the widow's heart to sing for *j*	Job 29:13	7442
and he shall see his face with *j*	Job 33:26	8643
all the sons of God shouted for *j*	Job 38:7	
is turned into *j* before him	Job 41:22	
let them ever shout for *j*	Ps 5:11	
in thy presence is fulness of *j*	Ps 16:11	8057
The king shall *j* thy strength	Ps 21:1	8055
in his tabernacle sacrifices of *j*	Ps 27:6	8643
but *j* cometh in the morning	Ps 30:5	7440
and shout for *j*, all ye that are	Ps 32:11	
Let them shout for *j*, and be glad	Ps 35:27	
house of God, with the voice of *j*	Ps 42:4	7440
of God, unto God my exceeding *j*	Ps 43:4	1524
the *j* of the whole earth, is	Ps 48:2	4885
Make me to hear *j* and gladness	Ps 51:8	8342
unto me the *j* of thy salvation	Ps 51:12	8342
they shout for *j*, they also sing	Ps 65:13	
the nations be glad and sing for *j*	Ps 67:4	
brought forth his people with *j*	Ps 105:43	8342
that sow in tears shall reap in *j*	Ps 126:5	7440
and let thy saints shout for *j*	Ps 132:9	7442
saints shall shout aloud for *j*	Ps 132:16	7442
not Jerusalem above my chief *j*	Ps 137:6	8057
to the counsellors of peace is *j*	Prov 12:20	8057
doth not intermeddle with his *j*	Prov 14:10	8057
Folly is *j* to him that is	Prov 15:21	
A man hath *j* by the answer of his	Prov 15:23	8057
and the father of a fool hath no *j*	Prov 17:21	8057
It is *j* to the just to do	Prov 21:15	8057
a wise child shall have *j* of him	Prov 23:24	8056
withheld not my heart from any *j*	Eccl 2:10	8057
sight wisdom, and knowledge, and *j*	Eccl 2:26	8057
him in the *j* of his heart	Eccl 5:20	8057
Go thy way, eat thy bread with *j*	Eccl 9:7	8057
nation, and not increased the *j*	Is 9:3	8057
they *j* before thee according to	Is 9:3	8055
according to the *j* in harvest	Is 9:3	8055
have no *j* in their young men	Is 9:17	8055
Therefore with *j* shall ye draw	Is 12:3	8342
j out of the plentiful field	Is 16:10	
And behold *j* and gladness, slaying	Is 22:13	8342
the *j* of the harp ceaseth	Is 24:8	4885
all *j* is darkened, the mirth of	Is 24:11	8057
increase their *j* in the LORD	Is 29:19	8057
houses of *j* in the joyous city	Is 32:13	4885
a *j* of wild asses, a pasture of	Is 32:14	4885
and rejoice even with *j* and	Is 35:2	1525
everlasting *j* upon their heads	Is 35:10	8057
they shall obtain *j* and gladness	Is 35:10	8057
j and gladness shall be found	Is 51:3	8342
everlasting *j* shall be upon their	Is 51:11	8057
they shall obtain gladness and *j*	Is 51:11	8057
Break forth into *j*, sing together	Is 52:9	
For ye shall go out with *j*	Is 55:12	8057
a *j* of many generations	Is 60:15	4885
the oil of *j* for mourning, the	Is 61:3	8342
everlasting *j* shall be unto them	Is 61:7	8057
shall sing for *j* of heart	Is 65:14	2898
a rejoicing, and her people a *j*	Is 65:18	4885
in Jerusalem, and *j* in my people	Is 65:19	7796
but he shall appear to your *j*	Is 66:5	8057
rejoice for *j* with her, all ye	Is 66:10	4885
and thy word was unto me the *j*	Jer 15:16	8342
I will turn their mourning into *j*	Jer 31:13	8342
And it shall be to me a name of *j*	Jer 33:9	8342
The voice of *j*, and the voice of	Jer 33:11	8342
of him, thou skippedst for *j*	Jer 48:27	
And *j* and gladness is taken from	Jer 48:33	8057
praise not left, the city of my *j*	Jer 49:25	4885

beauty, The *j* of the whole earth	Lam 2:15	4885
The *j* of our heart is ceased	Lam 5:15	4885
the *j* of their glory, the desire	Eze 24:25	4885
with the *j* of all their heart	Eze 36:5	8057
Rejoice not, O Israel, for *j*	Hos 9:1	1524
because *j* is withered away from	Joel 1:12	8342
cut off before our eyes, yea, *j*	Joel 1:16	8057
I will *j* in the God of my	Hab 3:18	1523
he will rejoice over thee with *j*	Zeph 3:17	8057
he will *j* over thee with singing	Zeph 3:17	1523
shall be to the house of Judah *j*	Zec 8:19	8342
rejoiced with exceeding great *j*	Mt 2:10	5479
word, and anon with *j* receiveth it	Mt 13:20	5479
for *j* thereof goeth and selleth	Mt 13:44	5479
enter thou into the *j* of thy lord	Mt 25:21	5479
enter thou into the *j* of thy lord	Mt 25:23	5479
sepulchre with fear and great *j*	Mt 28:8	5479
And thou shalt have *j* and gladness	Lk 1:14	5479
the babe leaped in my womb for *j*	Lk 1:44	20
bring you good tidings of great *j*	Lk 2:10	5479
ye in that day, and leap for *j*	Lk 6:23	5479
hear, receive the word with *j*	Lk 8:13	5479
the seventy returned again with *j*	Lk 10:17	5479
that likewise *j* shall be in	Lk 15:7	5479
there is *j* in the presence of the	Lk 15:10	5479
while they yet believed not for *j*	Lk 24:41	5479
to Jerusalem with great *j*	Lk 24:52	5479
that my *j* therefore is fulfilled	Jn 3:29	5479
that my *j* might remain in you, and	Jn 15:11	5479
that your *j* might be full	Jn 15:11	5479
sorrow shall be turned into *j*	Jn 16:20	5479
for *j* that a man is born into the	Jn 16:21	5479
your *j* no man taketh from you	Jn 16:22	5479
receive, that your *j* may be full	Jn 16:24	5479
have my *j* fulfilled in themselves	Jn 17:13	5479
me full of *j* with thy countenance	Acts 2:28	2167
And there was great *j* in that city	Acts 8:8	5479
the disciples were filled with *j*	Acts 13:52	5479
they caused great *j* unto all the	Acts 15:3	5479
I might finish my course with *j*	Acts 20:24	5479
but we also *j* in God through our	Rom 5:11	2744
and peace, and *j* in the Holy Ghost	Rom 14:17	5479
God of hope fill you with all *j*	Rom 15:13	5479
you with *j* by the will of God	Rom 15:32	5479
faith, but are helpers of your *j*	2Cor 1:24	5479
that my *j* is the *j* of you all	2Cor 2:3	5479
that my *j* is the *j* of you all	2Cor 2:3	5479
more joyed we for the *j* of Titus	2Cor 7:13	5479
the abundance of their *j* and their	2Cor 8:2	5479
fruit of the Spirit is love, *j*	Gal 5:22	5479
for you all making request with *j*	Phil 1:4	5479
your furtherance and *j* of faith	Phil 1:25	5479
Fulfil ye my *j*, that ye be	Phil 2:2	5479
and service of your faith, I *j*	Phil 2:17	5468
For the same cause also do ye *j*	Phil 2:18	5468
beloved and longed for, my *j*	Phil 4:1	5479
with *j* of the Holy Ghost	1Th 1:6	5479
For what is our hope, or *j*	1Th 2:19	5479
For ye are our glory and *j*	1Th 2:20	5479
for all the *j* wherewith we *j*	1Th 3:9	5479
for all the *j* wherewith we *j*	1Th 3:9	5468
that I may be filled with *j*	2Ti 1:4	5479
For we have great *j* and	Philem 7	5485
let me have *j* of thee in the Lord	Philem 20	3685
who for the *j* that was set before	Heb 12:2	5479
that they may do it with *j*	Heb 13:17	5479
count it all *j* when ye fall into	Jas 1:2	5479
mourning, and your *j* to heaviness	Jas 4:9	5479
ye rejoice with *j* unspeakable	1Pet 1:8	5479
may be glad also with exceeding *j*	1Pet 4:13	21
unto you, that your *j* may be full	1Jn 1:4	5479
to face, that our *j* may be full	2Jn 12	5479
I have no greater *j* than to hear	3Jn 4	5479
of his glory with exceeding *j*	Jude 24	20

JOYED

exceedingly the more *j* we for the	2Cor 7:13	5463

JOYFUL

king, and went unto their tents *j*	1Kin 8:66	8056
for the LORD had made them *j*	Ezr 6:22	8055
Then went Haman forth that day *j*	Est 5:9	8056
let no *j* voice come therein	Job 3:7	7445
that love thy name be *j* in thee	Ps 5:11	5970
And my soul shall be *j* in the LORD	Ps 35:9	1523
shall praise thee with *j* lips	Ps 63:5	7445
Make a *j* noise unto God, all ye	Ps 66:1	
make a *j* noise unto the God of	Ps 81:1	
the people that know the *j* sound	Ps 89:15	8643
let us make a *j* noise to the rock	Ps 95:1	
make a *j* noise unto him with	Ps 95:2	
Let the field be *j*, and all that	Ps 96:12	5937
Make a *j* noise unto the LORD, all	Ps 98:4	

5970: To jump.

7440: From 7442, creaking, shout for joy [cry, gladness, shouting, etc.].

7442: To creak [sing aloud, plus many other translations].

7445: From 7442, voice, singing.

7796: From 8321, a vine, wine (used in great rejoicing).

8055: To brighten up [merry].

8056: From 8055, to make merry [light-hearted].

8057: From 8056, glee [exceedingly joyful, festive].

8342: From 7797, cheerfulness [mirth, gladness].

8643: From 7321, split the ears; clangor of trumpets [jubilee, loud noise].

4. Now do the same thing for all the Greek words behind the English word joy in the New Testament. Record these words and their roots and definitions on the New Testament section of your study sheet.

New Testament

20: From 21, exultation [gladness].

21: To jump for joy [exceedingly glad].

2167: From 2165, put in a good frame of mind.

2744: To boast [glory, make boast].

3685: To derive pleasure from.

5463: Calmly happy, cheerful [greeting, hail, God-speed].

5479: From 5463, cheerfulness, calm delight.

5. In order to do an exhaustive study of joy, you must now do a simple and intermediate study of all the words in brackets above. You should be able to do this by following the step-by-step instructions in previous exercises in this book.

Just as there are many English words that express joy and happiness, so there are many Hebrew and Greek words in the Old and New Testaments that do the same thing. In English we derive pleasure from something, our face brightens, we smile with our eyes. We are happy. We grin, smile, chuckle, giggle, laugh, cry tears of joy, clap our hands, raise our arms, shout, jump up and down for joy, hug one another, join hands and dance and scream, bragging that our team is the best as we tear down the goal posts in joy.

Except for the goal posts, the people of Bible times rejoiced in just as many ways. Make a study of this progression of joy, returning to each passage above and its context, discerning at what level joy is being experienced and expressed.

AVOIDING WORD STUDY PITFALLS

Many unfortunate conclusions have been drawn from inadequate or incomplete word studies. As you conduct word studies, you need to avoid these mistakes and problems.

Perhaps the most common mistake is failing to study the text for what it says. Instead of letting the Bible speak to us, many of us approach the verses with the attitude, "I already know what this means." We fail to approach Bible study with an open and receptive mind. A good example of this is the word *baptism*. We automatically associate water with this word, no matter the context. Look up baptism in your *Strong's Exhaustive Concordance* and see if water will fit every context.

A second mistake is to be followers of a particular teacher and fail to read the text for ourselves. We should read the text for ourselves, learn from our teachers, but seek the Holy Spirit's guidance to apply the text to our lives.

Another problem is failing to put in the necessary effort for serious Bible study. Studying God's Word is a joy, but it yields its fruits to those who meditate on it day and night. We should read our Bible every day, attempting to grasp the meaning of what we read instead of mouthing words. We should not read for quantity or speed, but for the Holy Spirit to speak to us while we listen.

Another problem is reading books *about* the Bible instead of reading the Bible itself. Devotional books and other books about the Bible have their place, but nothing takes the place of reading the Bible itself. As you read, the Holy Spirit will begin to link verses with verses, explaining one text with another. Let the Bible itself become the best commentary on God's holy Word.

Using *Strong's* with Other Bible Reference Tools

In addition to *Strong's Exhaustive Concordance*, there are many excellent Bible reference tools available today: word study dictionaries, handbooks, commentaries, general Bible dictionaries, and study Bibles. In this chapter you will learn how to use your *Strong's* with some of these other Bible study tools. *Strong's* alone is a fine resource, but it becomes even more valuable when used along with these other study tools.

TWO SHORTCUT REFERENCE TOOLS

First, let's consider two *Strong's* shortcut reference tools that serve as valuable aids to Bible study.

The New Strong's™ Guide to Bible Words. Thomas Nelson Publishers has issued an English index to all the Hebrew and Greek words that appear in *Strong's Exhaustive Concordance*. These words, with short definitions of the Hebrew and Greek words behind the English, are integrated into one alphabetical listing for ease and convenience in word searching.

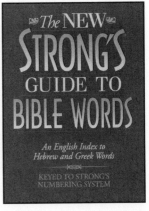

The NEW *STRONG'S* GUIDE TO BIBLE WORDS

An English Index to Hebrew and Greek Words

KEYED TO STRONG'S NUMBERING SYSTEM

Many steps in word searching can be eliminated by using *The New Strong's*™ *Guide to Bible Words*. First, you discern the English word in which you have an interest. Then, using this guide, you go directly to the English word for Strong's definitions.

The New Strong's™ *Complete Dictionary of Bible Words*. This reference book contains the same alphabetical English listing of words as *The New Strong's*™ *Guide to Bible Words*. It also contains all the features of Strong's Hebrew and Greek dictionaries—published in larger print for easier access.

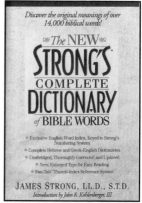

To use the *Complete Dictionary of Bible Words*, select the biblical word. Then look up the target word in English in the first part of the book. The *Strong's* number will be given for either the Hebrew or Greek dictionary. Proceed to the appropriate dictionary in the back of the book and you will find the complete *Strong's* entry, giving both Strong's italicized definitions and the King James translations of this word.

USING *STRONG'S* WITH A WORD STUDY DICTIONARY

A Bible word study dictionary focuses on defining special words in the Bible. The authors of such works probably used a text finder like *Strong's Concordance*, compiled a list of verses, and then wrote their dictionary based on those words. If you asked a Bible student what word study dictionary he knows about, he would probably mention *Vine's*. The *Vine's Complete Expository Dictionary of Old and New Testament Words*, published by Thomas Nelson, is a favorite among Bible students.

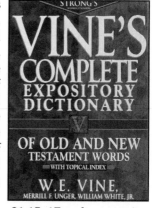

Let's assume that you are reading John 21:15–17 and you notice that Jesus questions Peter about his love for him. Peter is upset when Jesus asks him the third time about his love. Why? To find the answer, follow these steps:

1. Go to the main concordance section of *Strong's* and find the English word <u>love</u>. You glance down the columns to the New Testament references under <u>love</u>, <u>loved</u>, <u>lovedst</u>, <u>lovely</u>, <u>lover</u>, <u>lovers</u>, <u>love's</u>, <u>loves</u>, <u>lovest</u>, <u>loveth</u>, and <u>loving</u>. Without tallying the numbers for all these references, it is obvious that two Greek words predominate: 25 and 5368.

LOVED   867   **LOVERS**

L not the world, neither the 1Jn 2:15	25
If any man l the world 1Jn 2:15	25
the l of the Father is not in him 1Jn 2:15	26
what manner of l the Father hath 1Jn 3:1	26
that we should l one another 1Jn 3:11	25
because we l the brethren 1Jn 3:14	25
Hereby perceive we the l of God 1Jn 3:16	26
how dwelleth the l of God in him 1Jn 3:17	26
children, let us not l in word 1Jn 3:18	25
l one another, as he gave us 1Jn 3:23	25
Beloved, let us l one another 1Jn 4:7	25
for l is of God 1Jn 4:7	25
for God is l 1Jn 4:8	26
manifested the l of God toward us 1Jn 4:9	26
Herein is l, not that we loved 1Jn 4:10	26
we ought also to l one another 1Jn 4:11	25
If we l one another, God dwelleth 1Jn 4:12	25
us, and his l is perfected in us 1Jn 4:12	25
believed the l that God hath to.............. 1Jn 4:16	25
God is l 1Jn 4:16	26
dwelleth in l dwelleth in God 1Jn 4:16	26
Herein is our l made perfect 1Jn 4:17	26
There is no fear in l 1Jn 4:18	26
but perfect l casteth out fear 1Jn 4:18	26
feareth is not made perfect in l 1Jn 4:18	26
We l him, because he first loved............ 1Jn 4:19	25
l l God, and hateth his brother.............. 1Jn 4:20	25
how can he l God whom he hath not 1Jn 4:20	25
who loveth God l his brother also 1Jn 4:21	25
that we l the children of God 1Jn 5:2	25
children of God, when we l God............ 1Jn 5:2	26
For this is the l of God, that we 1Jn 5:3	26
children, which l l in the truth.............. 2Jn 1	25
Son of the Father, in truth and l 2Jn 3	26
beginning, that we l one another 2Jn 5	25
And this is l, that we walk after 2Jn 6	25
Gaius, whom I l in the truth 3Jn 1	25
Mercy unto you, and peace, and l .... Jude 2	26
Keep yourselves in the l of God .... Jude 21	25
thou hast left thy first l .... Rev 2:4	26
As many as I l, I rebuke and .... Rev 3:19	5368

LOVED

his wife; and he l her............................ Gen 24:67	157
And Isaac l Esau, because he did .... Gen 25:28	157
but Rebekah l Jacob.............................. Gen 25:28	157
meat, such as his father l .... Gen 27:14	157
And Jacob l Rachel................................ Gen 29:18	157
he l also Rachel more than Leah,.......... Gen 29:30	157
he l the damsel, and spake kindly .... Gen 34:3	157
Now Israel l Joseph more than all........ Gen 37:3	157
l him more than all his brethren .... Gen 37:4	157
because he l thy fathers,........................ Deut 4:37	157
But because the LORD l you.................. Deut 7:8	160
because the LORD thy God l thee .... Deut 23:5	157
Yea, he l the people .... Deut 33:3	2245
that he l a woman in the valley .... Judg 16:4	157
for he l Hannah 1Sa 1:5	157
and he l him greatly 1Sa 16:21	157
Jonathan l him as his own soul 1Sa 18:1	157
because he l him as his own soul 1Sa 18:3	160
But all Israel and Judah l David 1Sa 18:16	157
And Michal Saul's daughter l David 1Sa 18:20	157
that Michal Saul's daughter l him 1Sa 18:28	157
to swear again, because he l him 1Sa 20:17	160
for he l him as he 1Sa 20:17	157
him as he l his own soul........................ 1Sa 20:17	160
and the LORD l him 2Sa 12:24	157
and Amnon the son of David l her 2Sa 13:1	157
the love wherewith he had l her 2Sa 13:15	157
Solomon l the LORD, walking in 1Kin 3:3	157
the LORD l Israel for ever...................... 1Kin 10:9	157
But king Solomon l many strange 1Kin 11:1	157
the LORD hath l his people.................... 2Chr 2:11	160
because thy God l Israel, to.................... 2Chr 9:8	160
Rehoboam l Maachah the daughter 2Chr 11:21	157
for he l husbandry 2Chr 26:10	157
the king l Esther above all the .... Est 2:17	157
they whom I l are turned against .... Job 19:19	157
I have l the habitation of thy .... Ps 26:8	157
the excellency of Jacob whom he l........ Ps 47:4	157
Judah, the mount Zion which he l .... Ps 78:68	157
As he l cursing, so let it come .... Ps 109:17	157
thy commandments, which I have l...... Ps 119:47	157
thy commandments, which I have l...... Ps 119:48	157
been honourable, and I have l thee ...... Is 43:4	157
The LORD hath l him .... Is 48:14	157
for I have l strangers, and after .... Jer 2:25	157
host of heaven, whom they have l.......... Jer 8:2	157

Thus have they l to wander .... Jer 14:10	157
I have l thee with an everlasting .... Jer 31:3	157
and all them that thou hast l .... Eze 16:37	157
thou hast l a reward upon every .... Hos 9:1	157
were according as they l........................ Hos 9:10	157
Israel was a child, then I l him .... Hos 11:1	157
I have l you, saith the LORD.................. Mal 1:2	157
ye say, Wherein hast thou l us.............. Mal 1:2	157
yet I l Jacob,.. Mal 1:2	157
holiness of the LORD which he l .... Mal 2:11	157
Then Jesus beholding him l him .... Mk 10:21	25
for she l much .... Lk 7:47	25
For God so l the world, that he .... Jn 3:16	25
men l darkness rather than light,.......... Jn 3:19	25
Now Jesus l Martha, and her sister ...... Jn 11:5	25
the Jews, Behold how he l him.............. Jn 11:36	5368
For they l the praise of men more........ Jn 12:43	25
having l his own which were in .... Jn 13:1	25
the world, he l them unto the end .... Jn 13:1	25
of his disciples, whom Jesus l .... Jn 13:23	25
as I have l you, that ye also.................... Jn 13:34	25
loveth me shall be l of my Father .... Jn 14:21	25
If ye l me, ye would rejoice,.................. Jn 14:28	25
hath l me, so have I l you .... Jn 15:9	25
love one another, as I have l you.......... Jn 15:12	25
loveth you, because ye have l me.......... Jn 16:27	5368
thou hast sent me, and hast l them ...... Jn 17:23	25
as thou hast l me .... Jn 17:23	25
thou hast l me may be in them .... Jn 17:26	25
disciple standing by, whom he l .... Jn 19:26	25
the other disciple, whom Jesus l .... Jn 20:2	5368
whom Jesus l saith unto Peter .... Jn 21:7	25
disciple whom Jesus l following .... Jn 21:20	25
conquerors through him that l us.......... Rom 8:37	25
As it is written, Jacob have I l .... Rom 9:13	25
I love you, the less I be l 2Cor 12:15	25
faith of the Son of God, who l me .... Gal 2:20	25
his great love wherewith he l us .... Eph 2:4	25
in love, as Christ also hath l us .... Eph 5:2	26
even as Christ also l the church .... Eph 5:25	25
even our Father, which hath l us 2Th 2:16	25
having l this present world, and 2Ti 4:10	25
Thou hast l righteousness, and............ Heb 1:9	25
son of Bosor, who l the wages of 2Pet 2:15	25
Herein is love, not that we l God 1Jn 4:10	25
but that he l us 1Jn 4:10	25
Beloved, if God so l us, we ought.......... 1Jn 4:11	25
love him, because he first l us................ 1Jn 4:19	25
Unto him that l us, and washed us........ Rev 1:5	25
and to know that I have l thee .... Rev 3:9	25
they l not their lives unto the .... Rev 12:11	25

LOVEDST

thou l their bed where thou .... Is 57:8	157
for thou l me before the .... Jn 17:24	25

LOVELY

Saul and Jonathan were l and 2Sa 1:23	157
yea, he is altogether l .... Song 5:16	4261
a very l song of one that hath a .... Eze 33:32	5690
are pure, whatsoever things are l.......... Phil 4:8	4375

LOVER

for Hiram was ever a l of David............ 1Kin 5:1	157
L and friend hast thou put far .... Ps 88:18	157
But a l of hospitality .... Titus 1:8	5382
a l of good men, sober, just,.................. Titus 1:8	5358

LOVERS

My l and my friends stand aloof............ Ps 38:11	157
played the harlot with many l .... Jer 3:1	7453
thy l will despise thee, they.................... Jer 4:30	5689
for all thy l are destroyed...................... Jer 22:20	157
thy l shall go into captivity .... Jer 22:22	157
All thy l have forgotten thee .... Jer 30:14	157
among all her l she hath none to .... Lam 1:2	157
I called for my l, but they...................... Lam 1:19	157
givest thy gifts to all thy l .... Eze 16:33	157
through thy whoredoms with thy l .... Eze 16:36	157
therefore I will gather all thy l .... Eze 16:37	157
and she doted on her l, on the .... Eze 23:5	157
her into the hand of her l .... Eze 23:9	157
will raise up thy l against thee.............. Eze 23:22	157
she said, I will go after my l.................. Hos 2:5	157
And she shall follow after her l .... Hos 2:7	157
lewdness in the sight of her l .... Hos 2:10	157
rewards that my l have given me .... Hos 2:12	157
jewels, and she went after her l............ Hos 2:13	157
Ephraim hath hired l.............................. Hos 8:9	158
For men shall be l of their own 2Ti 3:2	5367
l of pleasures more than........................ 2Ti 3:4	5369

L

2. Entry 25 is *agapao* and 5368 is *phileo*. You read the italicized part of word 25 and consult the translation part. The English translation of a*gapao* is "love," referring to love on a social or moral level, a self-giving love. *Phileo* (5368) is defined as "friendship" and is translated as "kiss" or "love." This type of kiss is a sign between friends.

3. Now that you have completed your study in *Strong's,* you want to check the definitions and distinctions between the words. You pick up your copy of *Vine's Complete Expository Dictionary* and turn to love in the New Testament section. Incidentally, you will notice that love also is discussed in the Old Testament section and listed several times in the Topical Index. (See copy on following two pages.)

4. Notice that *Vine's* has a thorough discussion of both these words for love (*agapao*, 25; and *phileo*, 5368). You return to John 21:15-17 with new insights as gleaned from *Vine's.*

"So when they had dined, Jesus saith to Simon Peter, Simon, son of Jonas, lovest (*agapao*) thou me more than these? He saith unto him, Yea, Lord; thou knowest that I love (*phileo*) thee. He saith unto him, Feed my lambs. He saith to him again the second time, Simon, son of Jonas, lovest (*agapao*) thou me? He saith unto him, Yea, Lord; thou knowest that I love (*phileo*) thee. He saith unto him, Feed my sheep. He saith unto him the third time, Simon, son of Jonas, lovest (*phileo*) thou me? Peter was grieved because he said unto him the third time, Lovest (*phileo*) thou me? And he said unto him, Lord, thou knowest all things; thou knowest that I love (*phileo*) thee. Jesus saith unto him, Feed my sheep."

In his discussion with Peter, Jesus used the Greek word *agapao* two times. He was asking whether Peter had unselfish love that was ready and willing to serve. Finally, Jesus condescended to Peter's level of affection and asked, "Peter, do you love me even on the level of friendship?" This is when Peter got upset. Peter had vowed once that he would not deny Jesus, but he did. Would Peter fail Jesus again, even on a lower level of love?

Peter needed to forsake all and to follow Jesus with more than just tender affection. Great sacrifice takes great love that can come only from God. As history records, Peter did meet the challenge. He loved his Lord to the end with an *agapao* type of love.

LOSS   381   LOVE

Christ (see v. 13 with 2 Cor. 5:10); 2 Cor. 7:9, "(that) ye might suffer loss," RV (KJV, "might receive damage"); though the apostle did regret the necessity of making them sorry by his letter, he rejoiced that they were made sorry after a godly sort, which they would have done had their sorrow been otherwise than after a godly manner; in Phil. 3:8, "I suffered the loss (of all things)," RV, i.e., of all things which he formerly counted gain (especially those in verses 5 and 6, to which the article before "all things" points). See CAST, FORFEIT.¶

LOSS

1. *zēmia* (ζημία, 2209), akin to No. 2, above, is used in Acts 27:10, RV, "loss" (KJV, "damage"); v. 21, KJV and RV, "loss," of ship and cargo; in Phil. 3:7, 8 of the apostle's estimate of the things which he formerly valued, and of all things on account of "the excellency of the knowledge of Christ Jesus."¶

2. *apobolē* (ἀποβολή, 580), lit., "casting away" (*apo*, "away," *ballō*, "to cast"), is translated "loss" in Acts 27:22; in Rom. 11:15, "casting away," of the temporary exclusion of the nation of Israel from its position of divine favor, involving the reconciling of the world (i.e., the provision made through the gospel, which brings the world within the scope of reconciliation).¶

3. *hēttēma* (ἥττημα, 2275) denotes "a defect, loss," Rom. 11:12, RV, "loss," KJV, "diminishing" (for the meaning of which in regard to Israel see No. 2); 1 Cor. 6:7, RV, "defect" (KJV, "fault"). See DEFECT.

Note: For "suffer loss" see LOSE, No. 2.

LOT, LOTS

A. Noun.

klēros (κλῆρος, 2819) denotes (*a*) an object used in casting or drawing lots, which consisted of bits, or small tablets, of wood or stone (the probable derivation is from *klaō*, "to break"); these were sometimes inscribed with the names of persons, and were put into a receptacle or a garment ("a lap," Prov. 16:33), from which they were cast, after being shaken together; he whose "lot" first fell out was the one chosen. The method was employed in a variety of circumstances, e.g., of dividing or assigning property, Matt. 27:35; Mark 15:24; Luke 23:34; John 19:24 (cf., e.g., Num. 26:55); of appointing to office, Acts 1:26 (cf., e.g., 1 Sam. 10:20); for other occurrences in the OT, see, e.g., Josh. 7:14 (the earliest instance in Scripture); Lev. 16:7-10; Esth. 3:7; 9:24; (*b*) "what is obtained by lot, an allotted portion," e.g., of the ministry allotted

to the apostles, Acts 1:17, RV, "portion," marg., "lot" (KJV, "part"); in some mss. v. 25, KJV, "part" (the RV follows those which have *topos*, "place"); Acts 8:21; it is also used like *klēronomia*, "an inheritance," in Acts 26:18, of what God has in grace assigned to the sanctified; so Col. 1:12; in 1 Pet. 5:3 it is used of those the spiritual care of, and charge over, whom is assigned to elders, RV, "the charge allotted to you" (plural, lit., "the charges"), KJV, "(God's) heritage." From *klēros* the word "clergy" is derived (a transposition in the application of the term). See CHARGE, No. 4.¶

B. Verb.

lanchanō (λαγχάνω, 2975) denotes (*a*) "to draw lots," John 19:24; (*b*) "to obtain by lot, to obtain," Luke 1:9, "his lot was," lit., "he received by lot," i.e., by divine appointment; Acts 1:17, of the portion "allotted" by the Lord to His apostles in their ministry (cf. A, above); 2 Pet. 1:1, "that have obtained (a like precious faith)," i.e., by its being "allotted" to them, not by acquiring it for themselves, but by divine grace (an act independent of human control, as in the casting of "lots"). See OBTAIN.¶

Note: For divide by lot see DIVIDE.

LOUD

megas (μέγας, 3173), "great," is used, besides other meanings, of intensity, as, e.g., of the force of a voice, e.g., Matt. 27:46, 50; in the following the RV has "great" for the KJV, "loud," Rev. 5:2, 12; 6:10; 7:2, 10; 8:13; 10:3; 12:10; 14:7, 9, 15, 18. See GREAT.

LOVE (Noun and Verb)

A. Verbs.

1. *agapaō* (ἀγαπάω, 25) and the corresponding noun *agapē* (B, No. 1 below) present "the characteristic word of Christianity, and since the Spirit of revelation has used it to express ideas previously unknown, inquiry into its use, whether in Greek literature or in the Septuagint, throws but little light upon its distinctive meaning in the NT. Cf., however, Lev. 19:18; Deut. 6:5.

"*Agapē* and *agapaō* are used in the NT (*a*) to describe the attitude of God toward His Son, John 17:26; the human race, generally, John 3:16; Rom 5:8; and to such as believe on the Lord Jesus Christ, particularly, John 14:21; (*b*) to convey His will to His children concerning their attitude one toward another, John 13:34, and toward all men, 1 Thess. 3:12; 1 Cor. 16:14; 2 Pet. 1:7; (*c*) to express the essential nature of God, 1 John 4:8.

"Love can be known only from the actions it prompts. God's love is seen in the gift of His

(Page 381 from New Testament section of Nelson's edition of *Vine's*)

LOVE   382   LOVE FEASTS

Son, 1 John 4:9, 10. But obviously this is not the love of complacency, or affection, that is, it was not drawn out by any excellency in its objects, Rom. 5:8. It was an exercise of the divine will in deliberate choice, made without assignable cause save that which lies in the nature of God Himself, Cf. Deut. 7:7, 8.

"Love had its perfect expression among men in the Lord Jesus Christ, 2 Cor. 5:14; Eph. 2:4; 3:19; 5:2; Christian love is the fruit of His Spirit in the Christian, Gal. 5:22.

"Christian love has God for its primary object, and expresses itself first of all in implicit obedience to His commandments, John 14:15, 21, 23; 15:10; 1 John 2:5; 5:3; 2 John 6. Self-will, that is, self-pleasing, is the negation of love to God.

"Christian love, whether exercised toward the brethren, or toward men generally, is not an impulse from the feelings, it does not always run with the natural inclinations, nor does it spend itself only upon those for whom some affinity is discovered. Love seeks the welfare of all, Rom. 15:2, and works no ill to any, 13:8–10; love seeks opportunity to do good to 'all men, and especially toward them that are of the household of the faith,' Gal. 6:10. See further 1 Cor. 13 and Col. 3:12–14."*

In respect of *agapaō* as used of God, it expresses the deep and constant "love" and interest of a perfect Being towards entirely unworthy objects, producing and fostering a reverential "love" in them towards the Giver, and a practical "love" towards those who are partakers of the same, and a desire to help others to seek the Giver. See BELOVED.

2. *phileō* (φιλέω, 5368) is to be distinguished from *agapaō* in this, that *phileō* more nearly represents "tender affection." The two words are used for the "love" of the Father for the Son, John 3:35 (No. 1), and 5:20 (No. 2); for the believer, 14:21 (No. 1) and 16:27 (No. 2); both, of Christ's "love" for a certain disciple, 13:23 (No. 1), and 20:2 (No. 2). Yet the distinction between the two verbs remains, and they are never used indiscriminately in the same passage; if each is used with reference to the same objects, as just mentioned, each word retains its distinctive and essential character.

Phileō is never used in a command to men to "love" God; it is, however, used as a warning in 1 Cor. 16:22; *agapaō* is used instead, e.g., Matt. 22:37; Luke 10:27; Rom. 8:28; 1 Cor. 8:3; 1 Pet. 1:8; 1 John 4:21. The distinction between the two verbs finds a conspicuous instance in

the narrative of John 21:15–17. The context itself indicates that *agapaō* in the first two questions suggests the "love" that values and esteems (cf. Rev. 12:11). It is an unselfish "love," ready to serve. The use of *phileō* in Peter's answers and the Lord's third question, conveys the thought of cherishing the Object above all else, of manifesting an affection characterized by constancy, from the motive of the highest veneration. See also Trench, *Syn.*, §xii.

Again, to "love" (*phileō*) life, from an undue desire to preserve it, forgetful of the real object of living, meets with the Lord's reproof, John 12:25. On the contrary, to "love" life (*agapaō*) as used in 1 Pet. 3:10, is to consult the true interests of living. Here the word *phileō* would be quite inappropriate.

Note: In Mark 12:38, KJV, *thelō*, "to wish," is translated "love" (RV, "desire").

B. Nouns.

1. *agapē* (ἀγάπη, 26), the significance of which has been pointed out in connection with A, No. 1, is always rendered "love" in the RV where the KJV has "charity," a rendering nowhere used in the RV; in Rom. 14:15, where the KJV has "charitably," the RV, adhering to the translation of the noun, has "in love."

Note: In the two statements in 1 John 4:8 and 16, "God is love," both are used to enjoin the exercise of "love" on the part of believers. While the former introduces a declaration of the mode in which God's love has been manifested (vv. 9, 10), the second introduces a statement of the identification of believers with God in character, and the issue at the Judgment Seat hereafter (v. 17), an identification represented ideally in the sentence "as He is, so are we in this world."

2. *philanthrōpia* (φιλανθρωπία, 5363) denotes, lit., "love for man" (*phileō* and *anthrōpos*, "man"); hence, "kindness," Acts 28:2; in Titus 3:4, "(His) love toward man."¶ Cf. the adverb *philanthrōpōs*, "humanely, kindly," Acts 27:3.¶ See KINDNESS.

Note: For *philarguria*, "love of money," 1 Tim. 6:10, see MONEY (love of). For *philadelphia*, see BROTHER, *Note* (1).

LOVE FEASTS

agapē (ἀγάπη, 26) is used in the plural in Jude 12, and in some mss. in 2 Pet. 2:13; RV marg., "many ancient authorities read 'deceivings,'" (*apatais*); so the KJV. These love feasts arose from the common meals of the early churches (cf. 1 Cor. 11:21). They may have had this origin in the private meals of Jewish households, with the addition of the observance of the Lord's Supper. There were, however, similar

---

* From *Notes on Thessalonians*, by Hogg and Vine, p. 105.

(Page 382 from New Testament section of Nelson's edition of *Vine's*)

USING *STRONG'S* WITH BIBLE HANDBOOKS, COMMENTARIES, BIBLE DICTIONARIES, AND STUDY BIBLES

The resources above—handbooks, commentaries, dictionaries, and study Bibles—are alike in that they contribute greatly to serious study of the Bible. But each of these resources also has distinctive characteristics that set it apart from all the others.

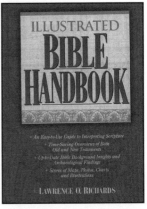

A Bible handbook, for example, is a one-volume guide to the Bible arranged around the books of the Bible, beginning with Genesis and continuing through Revelation. A handbook generally gives an overview of the contents of the books of the Bible without going into great detail on specific Bible passages. Many Bible handbooks contain charts, tables, maps, timelines, photographs, and other helpful study aids. A good example of a Bible handbook is the *Illustrated Bible Handbook,* published by Thomas Nelson.

The job of a commentary is to give detailed comments on specific passages of the Bible. But this Bible study tool comes in different forms, ranging from one-volume commentaries on the entire Bible to multi-volume commentary sets that may devote a full book in the series to one specific book of the Bible. *Nelson's New Illustrated Bible Commentary* is a good example of a one-volume work.

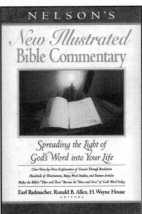

A Bible dictionary defines all the people, places, and things of the Bible in an alphabetical arrangement. Many Bible dictionaries also contain charts, photographs, and other graphic elements to enrich the Bible student's understanding of the life and times of the Bible. A good example of a Bible dictionary is *Nelson's New Illustrated Bible Dictionary.*

A study Bible is just what its name implies: a Bible with numerous study aids accompanying the Bible text to help the serious student learn more about the Scriptures. Typical features of a study Bible include commentary on the Bible text, Bible verse cross-references, an abbreviated concordance, maps, charts, and selected word studies. *The Nelson Study Bible* is a good example of a thorough and helpful resource with all these features.

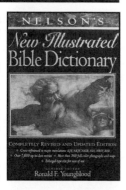

Each of these kinds of references can be used along with your *Strong's* to enhance your Bible study. Suppose you are reading in 2 Kings 5 about Naaman, the Syrian commander who went to the prophet Elisha to be healed of his leprosy. You want to know more about leprosy. Follow these steps:

1. In the main concordance section of *Strong's,* look up <u>leper</u> and its related words: <u>lepers</u>, <u>leprosy</u>, and <u>leprous</u>.

...all was the *l* of it ...					
and a half was the *l* thereof	Ex 37:6	753	gene... irom the mountains of ...	...ng 4:8	
two cubits was the *l* thereof	Ex 37:10	753	also are swifter than the *l*	Hab 1:8	5246
the *l* of it was a cubit, and the	Ex 37:25	753	**LEPER**		
five cubits was the *l* thereof	Ex 38:1	753	the *l* in whom the plague is, his	Lev 13:45	6879
and twenty cubits was the *l*	Ex 38:18	753	the *l* in the day of his cleansing	Lev 14:2	6879
a span was the *l* thereof, and a	Ex 39:9	753	of leprosy be healed in the *l*	Lev 14:3	6879
nine cubits was the *l* thereof	Deut 3:11	753	of the seed of Aaron is a *l*	Lev 22:4	6879
is thy life, and the *l* of thy days	Deut 30:20	753	they put out of the camp every *l*	Num 5:2	6879
which had two edges, of a cubit *l*	Judg 3:16	753	hath an issue, or that is a *l*	2Sa 3:29	6879
the *l* thereof was threescore	1Kin 6:2	753	man in valour, but he was a *l*	2Kin 5:1	6879
twenty cubits was the *l* thereof	1Kin 6:3	753	over the place, and recover the *l*	2Kin 5:11	6879
forepart was twenty cubits in *l*	1Kin 6:20	753	his presence a *l* as white as snow	2Kin 5:27	6879
four cubits was the *l* of one base	1Kin 7:2	753	so that he was a *l* unto the day	2Kin 15:5	6879
The *l* by cubits according to the	1Kin 7:6	753	Uzziah the king was a *l* unto the	2Chr 26:21	6879
the *l* of it was according to the	1Kin 7:27	753	in several house, being a *l*	2Chr 26:21	6879
the *l* whereof was according to	2Chr 3:4	753	for they said. He is a *l*	2Chr 26:23	6879
twenty cubits the *l* thereof	2Chr 3:8	753	And, behold, there came a *l*	Mt 8:2	3015
in *l* of days understanding	2Chr 4:1	753	in the house of Simon the *l*	Mt 26:6	3015
even *l* of days for ever and ever	Job 12:12	753	And there came a *l* to him.	Mk 1:40	3015
For *l* of days, and long life, and	Ps 21:4	753	in the house of Simon the *l*.	Mk 14:3	3015
L of days is in her right hand	Prov 3:2	753	**LEPERS**		
have him become his son at the *l*	Prov 3:16	753	And when these *l* came to the	2Kin 7:8	6879
in the *l* of his branches	Prov 29:21	319	Heal the sick, cleanse the *l*	Mt 10:8	3015
the *l* of the gates was the lower	Eze 31:7	753	the *l* are cleansed, and the deaf	Mt 11:5	3015
north, he measured the *l* thereof	Eze 40:11	753	many *l* were in Israel in the time	Lk 4:27	3015
the *l* thereof was fifty cubits,	Eze 40:20	753	the *l* are cleansed, the deaf hear	Lk 7:22	3015
the *l* was fifty cubits, and the	Eze 40:21	753	there met him ten men that were *l*	Lk 17:12	3015
the *l* was fifty cubits, and the	Eze 40:25	753	**LEPROSY**		
The *l* of the porch was twenty	Eze 40:36	753	of his flesh like the plague of *l*	Lev 13:2	6883
and he measured the *l* thereof	Eze 40:49	753	of his flesh, it is a plague of *l*	Lev 13:2	6883
So he measured the *l* thereof	Eze 41:2	753	it is a *l*	Lev 13:8	6883
the *l* thereof ninety cubits	Eze 41:4	753	When the plague of *l* is in a man	Lev 13:9	6883
he measured the *l* of the building	Eze 41:12	753	It is an old *l* in the skin of his	Lev 13:11	6883
high, and the *l* thereof two cubits	Eze 41:15	753	if a *l* break out abroad in the	Lev 13:12	6883
the *l* thereof, and the walls	Eze 41:22	753	the *l* cover all the skin of him	Lev 13:12	6883
Before the *l* of an hundred cubits	Eze 41:22	753	if the *l* have covered all his	Lev 13:13	6883
the *l* thereof was fifty cubits	Eze 42:2	753	it is a *l*	Lev 13:15	6883
For the *l* of the chambers that	Eze 42:7	753	it is a plague of *l* broken out of	Lev 13:20	6883
the *l* shall be the *l* of five	Eze 42:8	753	it is a *l* broken out of the	Lev 13:25	6883
the sanctuary five hundred in *l*	Eze 45:1	753	it is the plague of *l*	Lev 13:25	6883
shalt thou measure the *l* of five	Eze 45:2	753	it is the plague of *l*	Lev 13:27	6883
the five and twenty thousand of *l*	Eze 45:3	753	even a *l* upon the head or beard	Lev 13:30	6883
the *l* shall be over against one	Eze 45:5	753	it is a *l* sprung up in his bald	Lev 13:42	6883
in *l* as one of the other parts,	Eze 45:7	753	as the *l* appeareth in the skin of	Lev 13:43	6883
of five and twenty thousand in *l*	Eze 48:8	753	also that the plague of *l* is in	Lev 13:47	6883
five and twenty thousand in *l*	Eze 48:9	753	it is a plague of *l*, and shall be	Lev 13:49	6883
five and twenty thousand in *l*	Eze 48:10	753	the plague is a fretting *l*	Lev 13:51	6883
have five and twenty thousand in *l*	Eze 48:13	753	for it is a fretting *l*	Lev 13:52	6883
all the *l* shall be five and twenty	Eze 48:13	753	of *l* in a garment of woollen or	Lev 13:59	6883
the residue in *l* over against the	Eze 48:18	753	if the plague of *l* be healed in	Lev 14:3	6883
			cleansed from the *l* seven times	Lev 14:7	6883
			of him in whom the plague of *l*	Lev 14:32	6883

LEPROUS	794			LEVI	
I put the plague of *l* in a house	Lev 14:34	6883	sent *l* by posts on horseback, and	Est 8:10	5612
it is a fretting *l* in the house	Lev 14:44	6883	sent *l* unto all the Jews that	Est 9:20	5612
law for all manner of plague of *l*	Lev 14:54	6883	he commanded by *l* that his wicked	Est 9:25	5612
for the *l* of a garment, and of a	Lev 14:55	6883	he sent the *l* unto all the Jews,	Est 9:30	5612
this is the law of *l*	Lev 14:57	6883	Baladan, king of Babylon, sent *l*	Is 39:1	5612
Take heed in the plague of *l*	Deut 24:8	6883	Because thou hast sent *l* in thy	Jer 29:25	5612
for he would recover man of his *l*	2Kin 5:3	6883	written over him in *l* of Greek	Lk 23:38	1121
thou mayest recover him of his *l*	2Kin 5:6	6883	saying, How knoweth this man *l*	Jn 7:15	1121
unto me to recover a man of his *l*	2Kin 5:7	6883	desired of him *l* to Damascus to	Acts 9:2	1992
The *l* therefore of Naaman shall	2Kin 5:27	6883	they wrote *l* by them after this	Acts 15:23	
the *l* even rose up in his	2Chr 26:19	6883	I received *l* unto the brethren	Acts 22:5	1992
And immediately his *l* was cleansed	Mt 8:3	3014	We neither received *l* out of	Acts 28:21	1121
immediately the *l* departed from	Mk 1:42	3014	ye shall approve by your *l*	1Cor 16:3	1992
city, behold a man full of *l*	Lk 5:12	3014	or *l* of commendation from you	2Cor 3:1	
immediately the *l* departed from	Lk 5:13	3014	as if I would terrify you by *l*	2Cor 10:9	1992
LEPROUS			For his *l*, say they, are weighty	2Cor 10:10	1992
behold, his hand was *l* as snow	Ex 4:6	6879	in word by *l* when we are absent	2Cor 10:11	1992
He is a *l* man, he is unclean	Lev 13:44	6879	**LETTEST**		
and, behold, Miriam became *l*	Num 12:10	6879	*l* such words go out of thy mouth	Job 15:13	
Miriam, and, behold, she was *l*	Num 12:10	6879	with a cord which thou *l* down	Job 41:1	8257
there were four *l* men at the	2Kin 7:3	6879	now *l* thou thy servant depart in	Lk 2:29	630
he was *l* in his forehead, and they	2Chr 26:20	6879	**LETTETH**		
LESHEM *(le'shem)* See Laish. *Same as Laish.*			hands escape, he that *l* him go	2Kin 10:24	
of Dan went up to fight against *L*	Josh 19:47	3959	strife is as when one *l* out water	Prov 17:14	6362
it, and dwelt therein, and called *L*	Josh 19:47	3959	only he who now *l* will let	2Th 2:7	2722
LESS See Appendix.			**LETTING** See Letushim.		
LESSER See Appendix.			**LETUSHIM** *(le·tu'·shim)* A son of Dedan.		
LEST See Appendix.			sons of Dedan were Asshurim, and *L*	Gen 25:3	3912
LET See Appendix.			**LETUSHITES** See Letushim.		
LETHEK See Homer.			**LEUMMIM** *(le·um'·mim)* A son of Dedan.		
LETTER			were Asshurim, and Letushim, and *L*	Gen 25:3	3817
			LEVI *(le'·vi)* See Levite, Levitical, Matthew.		

2. Notice the two Hebrew words behind Naaman's disease are 6879 and 6883. Turn to these two words in the Hebrew dictionary section of *Strong's*.

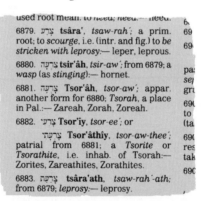

used root mean. to need; need. — need. 6...

6879. צָרַע **tsara'**, *tsaw-rah'*; a prim. root; to *scourge*, i.e. (intr. and fig.) to *be stricken with leprosy*:— leper, leprous.

6880. צִרְעָה **tsir'âh**, *tsir-aw'*; from 6879; a *wasp* (as *stinging*):— hornet.

6881. צָרְעָה **Tsor'âh**, *tsor-aw'*; appar. another form for 6880; *Tsorah*, a place in Pal.:— Zareah, Zorah, Zoreah.

6882. צָרְעִי **Tsor'îy**, *tsor-ee'*; or

צָרְעָתִי **Tsor'âthîy**, *tsor-aw-thee'*; patrial from 6881; a *Tsorite* or *Tsorathite*, i.e. inhab. of Tsorah:— Zorites, Zareathites, Zorathites.

6883. צָרַעַת **tsâra'ath**, *tsaw-rah'-ath*; from 6879; *leprosy*:— leprosy.

3. Notice that word 6883 comes from the root word 6879, meaning "to scourge, to be stricken with leprosy." This doesn't yield any information about the nature of the disease, so back you go to the main concordance section of *Strong's* for further research. This time you look for the New Testament Greek word or words translated as "leper" or "leprosy." You find one word, number 3015. Turn to this word in *Strong's* Greek dictionary.

*un-
*):—

3012. λέντιον *lention, ten -tee-on; or* Lat. or., a *"linon"* oloth, i.o. *apron;* towel.

; of
:e:—

3013. λεπίς **lĕpis,** *lep-is´;* from λέπω **lĕpō** (to *peel*); a *flake:*— scale.

a
'erb,
:her
s; to
;un-

3014. λέπρα **lĕpra,** *lep´-rah;* from the same as 3013; *scaliness,* i.e. *"leprosy":*— leprosy.

3015. λεπρός **lĕprŏs,** *lep-ros´;* from the same as *3014;* *scaly,* i.e. *leprous* (a *leper):*— leper.

'-o;

3016. λεπτόν **lĕptŏn,** *lep-ton´;* neut. of a der. of the same as *3013;* something

4. You see that entry word 3015 comes from word 3014 (meaning "scaliness"), which in turn comes from word 3013 (meaning "to peel" or "a flake"). You begin to realize that leprosy involved a peeling, flaking, or scaling—probably of the skin. Back you go to the main concordance section of *Strong's* for further research. This time you notice that leprosy is referred to numerous times in the thirteenth and fourteenth chapters of Leviticus.

there met him ten men that were *l*	Lk 17:12	3015

LEPROSY

of his flesh like the plague of *l*	Lev 13:2	6883
of his flesh, it is a plague of *l*	Lev 13:3	6883
it is a *l*	Lev 13:8	6883
When the plague of *l* is in a man	Lev 13:9	6883
It is an old *l* in the skin of his	Lev 13:11	6883
if a *l* break out abroad in the	Lev 13:12	6883
the *l* cover all the skin of him	Lev 13:12	6883
if the *l* have covered all his	Lev 13:13	6883
it is a *l*	Lev 13:15	6883
it is a plague of *l* broken out of	Lev 13:20	6883
it is a *l* broken out of the	Lev 13:25	6883
it is the plague of *l*	Lev 13:25	6883
it is the plague of *l*	Lev 13:27	6883
even a *l* upon the head or beard	Lev 13:30	6883
it is a *l* sprung up in his bald	Lev 13:42	6883
as the *l* appeareth in the skin of	Lev 13:43	6883
also that the plague of *l* is in	Lev 13:47	6883
it is a plague of *l*, and shall be	Lev 13:49	6883
the plague is a fretting *l*	Lev 13:51	6883
for it is a fretting *l*	Lev 13:52	6883
of *l* in a garment of woollen or	Lev 13:59	6883
if the plague of *l* be healed in	Lev 14:3	6883
cleansed from the *l* seven times	Lev 14:7	6883
of him in whom is the plague of *l*	Lev 14:32	6883

5. With your Bible open to Leviticus 13, you turn to the commentary on this chapter in *Nelson's New Illustrated Bible Commentary.* You find several illuminating paragraphs about leprosy, the nature of this disease, and the fate of those who contracted this malady. Note that an "In Depth" feature on page 172 summarizes what we know about the disease.

IN DEPTH | **Leprosy**

Leprosy (Lev. 13:12) was one of the most feared diseases in the ancient world. Lepers suffered from a slowly progressing, ordinarily incurable skin disease that was believed to be highly contagious. As a result, anyone who appeared to have leprosy, even if the symptoms were caused by some other condition, was banished from the community.

True leprosy is caused by a bacterium that spreads across the skin, creating sores, scabs, and white shining spots. The most serious problem, however, is a loss of sensation. Without the ability to feel, lepers injure their tissue, leading to further infection, deformity, muscle loss, and eventual paralysis. Fortunately, modern medicine has all but eliminated the disease.

The Law was quite detailed in its instructions regarding recognition and quarantine of leprous persons. Priests became the central figures for diagnosis, care of patients, and taking sanitary precautions to protect the rest of the community. The Law required that a leper be isolated from the rest of society (Lev. 13:45, 46). Infected persons were required to wear mourning clothes, leave their hair in disorder, keep their beards covered, and cry 'Unclean! Unclean!' so that others could avoid them. Any contact would defile the person who touched a leper.

Sometimes lepers were miraculously cured, as in the case of Moses (Ex. 4:7), his sister Miriam (Num. 12:10), and Naaman (2 Kin. 5:1, 10), and Jesus healed lepers as a sign to vindicate His ministry. On one occasion He healed ten of them but only one returned to thank Him (Luke 17:11–15).

6. From these comments you learn that *leprosy* was a word used for many infectious skin diseases. A person diagnosed with this malady was required to live apart from others to keep from spreading the disease. Leviticus 14 explains the ritual required for cleansing a healed leper.

7. For further information about leprosy, you turn to the entry <u>leprosy</u> in *Nelson's New Illustrated Bible Dictionary*. Then note the subject also is dealt with within a discussion of "Diseases of the Bible" beginning on page 358.

LEGACY — an inheritance (Prov. 3:35).

LEGION — the principal unit of the Roman army, consisting of 3,000 to 6,000 infantry troops and 100 to 200 cavalrymen. The New Testament does not use the word "legion" in its strict military sense, but in a general sense to express a large number. When Jesus healed a man possessed by unclean spirits or demons, He asked the man his name. He replied, "My name is Legion; for we are many" (Mark 5:9). The man was inhabited by many demons.

LEHABIM [lih HAY bim] — a son of Mizraim (Gen. 10:13).

LEHI [LEE high] (*jawbone*) — a place in the hill country of Judah (Judg. 15:9, 14, 19) where

LEOPARD (see ANIMALS OF THE BIBLE).

LEPROSY — a slowly progressing and incurable skin disease. In the Bible the word "leprosy" refers to a variety of symptoms. Modern medicine now recognizes that some of these symptoms belonged to diseases other than leprosy.

There are several types of leprosy. Biblical leprosy was most likely a severe type of psoriasis, a form of the disease relatively rare in modern times.

Old Testament Law was quite detailed in its instructions regarding recognition and quarantine of leprous persons. The Bible never implies that leprosy can be cured by nonmiraculous means, even though it does contain guidelines for readmitting cured lepers into normal society. The Old Testament contains no references to treatment or remedy. Jehoram's exclamation "Am I God, to kill and make alive, that this man sends a man to me to heal him of his leprosy?" (2 Kin. 5:7) implies the belief that leprosy could be cured only by a miracle.

Leprosy is a chronic, infectious disease characterized by sores, scabs, and white shining spots beneath the skin. Modern medicine has all but eliminated the disease after learning proper methods of treatment.

The Mosaic Law was very specific about the proper methods of purification where leprosy was concerned. The priest was the central figure in the Old Testament regulations for the care of patients and for sanitary precautions.

If the symptoms of leprosy showed up in a person, the priest was to decide if this was leprosy or some other disease. Because of the need to control the spread of a disease for which there was no cure, the law required that a leper be isolated from the rest of society (Lev. 13:45–46). While thus excluded, lepers were required to wear mourning clothes, leave their hair in disorder and cry "Unclean! Unclean!" so everyone could avoid them.

Leprosy in a house showed up in a greenish or reddish color on the walls. When the owner of a house noticed these symptoms, he reported them to the priest. The priest purified the dwelling if the disease could be controlled, or he ordered it destroyed if the signs of leprosy lingered on (Lev. 14:33–53).

In Old Testament times, linen and woolen garments were also said to be leprous when they had patches of mildew, mold, or fungus growth (Lev. 13:47–59). Leprosy in clothes, fabrics, and leather was also indicated by greenish or reddish spots. These spots were reported to the priest, who ordered the affected article to be purified or burned (Lev. 13:47–59).

Any contact with lepers defiled the persons who touched them. Sometimes leprosy victims were miraculously cured. Moses (Ex. 4:7), Miriam, his sister (Num. 12:10), and Naaman (2 Kin. 5:1, 10) are prominent examples of such miracles.

King Uzziah was a leper from middle age until death (2 Chr. 26:19–21). The leprosy inflicted upon him (2 Kin. 15:5; 2 Chr. 26:23) for his unwarranted assumption of the priesthood began in his forehead.

In the New Testament, cleansing of lepers is mentioned as a specific portion of Jesus' work of healing. On one occasion Jesus healed ten lepers, but only one returned to thank him (Luke 17:11–15).

Also see DISEASES OF THE BIBLE.

LESHEM [LESH uhm] — a form of LAISH.

LETTERS — written messages between persons separated by distance. In the Old Testament David wrote a letter to Joab, sending Uriah the Hittite into the heat of battle and insuring his death. In Bible times, letters were written on sheets of PARCHMENT, or animal skins; fragments of pottery; papyrus; and clay tablets.

In the New Testament, Saul of Tarsus went to the high priest in Jerusalem and secured letters from him to the synagogues of Damascus. These letters authorized Saul to arrest Christians and bring them to Jerusalem (Acts 9:2; 22:5). The Jerusalem Council also sent a letter to Christians expressing their decision (Acts 15:23, 30).

Also see EPISTLE; WRITING; WRITING MATERIALS.

LETUSHIM [lih TOO shuhm] — a son of Dedan (Gen. 25:3).

LEUMMIM [LEE uh mim] (*people*) — a son of Dedan (Gen. 25:3).

LEVI [LEE vigh] (*joined*) — the name of four men and one tribe in the Bible:

1. The third son of Jacob and Leah (Gen. 29:34). His three sons were ancestors of the three main divisions of the Levitical priesthood: the GERSHONITES, the KOHATHITES, and the MERARITES (Gen. 46:11). Levi participated in the plot against Joseph (Gen. 37:4) and later took his family to Egypt with Jacob. On his deathbed Jacob cursed Simeon and Levi because of their "cruelty" and "wrath," and foretold that their descendants would be divided and scattered (Gen. 49:5–7). Levi died in Egypt at the age of 137 (Ex. 6:16).

2. A tribe descended from Levi (Ex. 6:19). Also see LEVITES.

3. Another name for MATTHEW, one of the twelve apostles (Mark 2:14). Levi was formerly a tax collector.

4. An ancestor of Jesus Christ (Luke 3:24). Levi was a son of Melchi and the father of Matthat.

5. Another ancestor of Jesus Christ (Luke 3:29). This Levi was a son of Simeon and the father of Matthat.

(Page 760 from *Nelson's New Illustrated Bible Dictionary*)

DISEASES OF THE BIBLE 358

Botch (see *Boils*).

Bowels, Disease of (see *Dysentery*).

Cancer. This disease is mentioned only once in the Bible: "And their message will spread like cancer" (2 Tim. 2:17; canker, KJV; gangrene, NASB, REB, NIV, NRSV). It refers to the circulatory deterioration known as gangrene, which spreads rapidly and eats up tissue.

Canker (see *Cancer*).

Consumption. Moses warned the rebellious Israelites, "The LORD shall smite thee with a consumption, and with a fever, and with an inflammation and with an extreme burning" (Deut. 28:22; wasting disease, NIV). This disease is probably tuberculosis, a consumptive infection of the lungs.

Dropsy. This describes an abnormal accumulation of serous fluid in the body's connective tissue or in a serous cavity. The accumulation causes swelling. Jesus met at least one victim of dropsy in a certain Pharisee's house. Asked by Jesus if he thought it lawful to heal on the Sabbath, the Pharisee declined to answer. Jesus then healed the sufferer (Luke 14:1–4).

Dumbness (see *Muteness*).

Dumb Spirit (see *Mute Spirit*).

Dysentery. This is a disease that rots the bowels, or the intestines, in its advanced stage (2 Chr. 21:15–19). The fibrine separates from the inner coating of the intestines and is expelled. The KJV refers to a severe form of dysentery as the bloody flux. The father of a Christian named Publius lay sick with this disease (Acts 28:8). Paul prayed for him and the man was healed. Some scholars believe dysentery was also the strange malady that afflicted King Hezekiah of Judah (2 Kin. 20:1).

Eczema. A symptom of this disease was an inflammation of the skin, marked by redness, itching, and oozing lesions that become scaly, encrusted, or hardened (Lev. 21:20; 22:22; scurvy, KJV; itching disease, NRSV; festering sores, NIV).

Emerod (see *Tumor*).

Epilepsy (see *Mute Spirit*).

Feet, Diseased. Excessive uric acid in the blood causes this kidney ailment that manifests itself through painful inflammation of joints. Second Chronicles 16:12 says that King Asa had a foot disease, which apparently was gout.

Fever. The KJV uses the word "ague" to describe a burning fever. Moses warned the rebellious Israelites that "I will even appoint over you terror, consumption and the burning ague, that shall consume the eyes" (Lev. 26:16).

When Jesus found Simon Peter's mother-in-law ill with this symptom, He rebuked the fever and she was able to rise from her bed and wait on the disciples (Luke 4:38–39). On another occasion, Jesus healed the feverish son of a government official (John 4:46–54). Many diseases in ancient Israel would have been characterized by high fevers, the most common of which were malaria and typhoid.

Gangrene (see *Cancer*).

Hemorrhage (see *Blood, Flow of*).

Insanity. King Saul seems to have had symptoms of manic depression (1 Sam. 16:14–23), and the Bible mentions others who may have suffered from mental or nervous disorders. King Nebuchadnezzar is an example (Dan. 4:33). The words "mad" and "madness" are also used by various translations to refer to this malady (Deut. 28:28; NKJV, KJV, NIV).

Intestines, Disease of (see *Dysentery*).

Itch. This is a curse which God threatened to send upon the Hebrew people if they departed from faith in Him (Deut. 28:27). Itch is caused by a microscopic mite that burrows into the skin, causing extreme discomfort.

Itching Disease (see *Eczema*)

Leprosy. One of the most dreaded diseases of the world, leprosy is caused by a bacillus and is

A blind harpist practicing his skill, from an early Egyptian tomb carving.

(Page 358 from *Nelson's New Illustrated Bible Dictionary*)

Getting the Most from Your *New Strong's™* Concordance

characterized by formation of nodules that spread, causing loss of sensation and deformity. Now treated with sulfone drugs, leprosy is perhaps the least infectious of all known contagious diseases. Hansen's Disease, as it is more properly known, was only one of various skin diseases afflicting people in Old Testament times, all of them referred to by the same Hebrew word (Lev. 13).

On the basis of a hair in a scab, a pimple, or a spot on the skin that had turned white, the priest would declare a person to be a leper and would quarantine him for seven days. If no change in the spot occurred by then, the quarantine would be extended another week. At that time, if the spot had started to fade, the "leper" would be pronounced cured and returned to his normal life. However, if the spot remained or had spread, he was declared unclean and banished. The words scurf and scall are applied to these spots on the skin by various English translations of the Bible (Lev. 13:30).

Skin diseases were very common in the Near East. Israelites who were healed of them were expected to offer certain sacrifices and engage in rites of purification (Lev. 14:1–32). Jesus healed lepers on numerous occasions (Luke 5:12–13; 17:12–17).

Lunacy, Lunatick (see *Mute Spirit*).

partial or total paralysis. The Gospels record a well-known incident in which Jesus healed a paralyzed man at Capernaum (Mark 2:1–12) The Book of Acts describes how the apostles healed people with this disease (Acts 8:7; 9:33–34; palsy, KJV).

Scabs (see *Boils*)

Scall (see *Leprosy*).

Scurf (see *Leprosy*).

Scurvy (see *Eczema*).

Sores (see *Boils*).

Tumor. The specific nature of this disease is unknown, although some scholars believe the word refers to hemorrhoids (Deut. 28:27; 1 Sam. 6:11). Other versions prefer ulcers (NRSV) or emerods (KJV).

Ulcer (see *Tumor*).

Wasting Disease (see *Consumption*).

Worms. The prophet Isaiah warned that the rebellious people of Israel would be afflicted with worms (Is. 51:8). He also predicted this fate for Babylon (Is. 14:11). This parasitic disease could be fatal because no medical remedies were available. Worms such as tapeworms and hookworms live as parasites in the human body and cause illness and disease.

The Bible says that "an angel of the Lord" struck Herod the Great. Worms ate him up and he died (Acts 12:23).

8. From the dictionary article you learn that "leprosy is a chronic, infectious disease characterized by sores, scabs, and white shining spots beneath the skin. Modern medicine has all but eliminated the disease after learning proper methods of treatment." You also learn that other prominent persons in the Bible besides Naaman who suffered from this dread disease were Moses, Miriam, and King Uzziah.

9. When you looked under <u>leper</u> in the main concordance section of *Strong's,* you noticed there were a couple of New Testament passages where Jesus dealt with lepers. The first is Matthew 8:2.

also are swifter than the *l*	Hab 1:8	524(
LEPER		
the *l* in whom the plague is, his	Lev 13:45	6879
the *l* in the day of his cleansing	Lev 14:2	6879
of leprosy be healed in the *l*	Lev 14:3	6879
of the seed of Aaron is a *l*	Lev 22:4	6879
they put out of the camp every *l*	Num 5:2	6879
hath an issue, or that is a *l*	2Sa 3:29	6879
man in valour, but he was a *l*	2Kin 5:1	6879
over the place, and recover the *l*	2Kin 5:11	6879
his presence a *l* as white as snow	2Kin 5:27	6879
so that he was a *l* unto the day	2Kin 15:5	6879
Uzziah the king was a *l* unto the	2Chr 26:21	6879
in a several house, being a *l*	2Chr 26:21	6879
for they said, He is a *l*	2Chr 26:23	6879
And, behold, there came a *l*	Mt 8:2	3015
in the house of Simon the *l*	Mt 26:6	3015
And there came a *l* to him,	Mk 1:40	3015
in the house of Simon the *l*	Mk 14:3	3015
LEPERS		
And when these *l* came to the	2Kin 7:8	6879

10. You look up Matthew 8:2 in your *Nelson Study Bible* and find there a brief note on this instance of Jesus healing a leper.

7:21–23 Because so **many** people teach the wrong way, there is a tendency to ask how so many people could be wrong. Such doubts are especially strong when false teachers prophesy, cast out demons, and perform wonders in Jesus' **name**. However, it is important to remember that the Word of God is superior to any miracle. **7:24–27** The key difference in the two houses is not their external appearance. Pharisees and scribes may seem to be as righteous as the heirs of the kingdom. The key in the story is the foundations. The **house on the rock** pictures a life founded on a proper relationship to Christ (16:18; 1 Cor. 10:4; 1 Pet. 2:4–8). It will stand the test of Christ's judgment, but the **house on the sand** will fail the test (see 1 Cor. 3:12–15). **7:29 not as the scribes:** Scribes would often cite authorities in order to lend credence to their statements. Jesus' words were self-authenticating. Note His phrase "I say to you" in 5:20, 22, 26, 28, 32.
8:2, 3 Before this miracle, the only record of an Israelite being healed of leprosy was the case of Miriam in Num. 12:10–15. The phrase **if You are willing** is important because it indicates genuine faith. It does not necessarily mean that if one simply believes, God *will* do something, but that He *can* do it (see Dan. 3:17, 18). Normally, touching a leper would result in ceremonial defilement (see Lev. 14:45, 46;

19	ª[John 15:2, 6]
21	ªLuke 6:46
	ᵇRom. 2:13
22	ªNum. 24:4
23	ª[2 Tim. 2:19]
	ᵇPs. 5:5; 6:8ꞔ
24	ªLuke 6:47–49
28	ªMatt. 13:54
29	ª[John 7:46]
	CHAPTER 8
2	ªMark 1:40–45
	ᵇJohn 9:38
3	ªLuke 4:27
4	ªMark 5:43
	ᵇLuke 5:14
	ꞔDeut. 24:8
5	ªLuke 7:1–3
	ᵇMatt. 27:54
8	ªLuke 15:19, 21
	ᵇPs. 107:20

Num. 5:2, 3; Deut. 24:8). In this case, Jesus touched the leper, and the leper became clean. **8:4 See that you tell no one:** Perhaps Jesus gave this command so that the healed person would first obey the Law before he became preoccupied with telling others about his healing. Jesus' command to **show yourself to the priest** involved no small undertaking for the cleansed leper. He would need to make the journey from near the Sea of Galilee to Jerusalem, and there offer the sacrifice required by Moses (see Lev. 14:4–32). The purpose of Christ's command was not only to obey the Law of Moses, but also to be a testimony to the religious authorities in Jerusalem that the Messiah had arrived. Jesus also commanded the man to keep quiet because He did not want the Jewish people to act too hastily on preconceived, erroneous ideas of the Messiah and His kingdom (see John 6:14, 15).
8:5–9 In the New Testament, centurions (officers in charge of one hundred soldiers) are consistently looked upon in a favorable light. These soldiers were the equivalent of a present-day sergeant. The centurion's response to Jesus indicated his clear understanding of **authority**.
8:10 He marveled: Only one other time does Scripture say Jesus marveled: when His own townspeople rejected Him (Mark 6:6). **I have not found . . . not even in Israel:**

11. At Matt. 8:2 in the text of the *Nelson Study Bible*, you notice there is a cross-reference to Mark 1:40–45. When you turn to these verses you quickly discover that this is Mark's parallel account of the healing of the same leper.

1:41 Jesus was **moved with compassion.** He not only healed but touched the leper. How often do we see the need but remain unmoved and uninvolved? Scripture has over four hundred passages admonishing us to care for the poor (see 8:2; Lev. 15:7–11). **1:44** After healing the leper, Jesus commanded him to **say nothing to anyone.** His demand for silence has several plausible explanations. (1) The report of Jesus' healing the man may have prejudiced the priest who needed to pronounce him clean. (2) Jesus did not want to be known primarily as a miracle worker, so He often commanded those who received His healing to remain quiet. (3) The man's testimony would possibly have hastened the confrontation between Jesus and the religious leaders. **1:45** The cleansed leper did not obey Jesus' simple injunction to keep quiet. As a result, Jesus had to remain in **deserted places** because the crowds swarmed to Him. **2:1–28** Mark's first chapter establishes Jesus as a popular figure who experiences great success. Chapters 2 and 3 demonstrate rising opposition to His mission and teaching and suggest more drama and suspense to come. **2:2** Mark is largely a record of Christ's actions, but what Jesus said is not neglected. Here he describes how Jesus **preached the word,** the message of the coming kingdom. **2:4** Many in the crowd may have come expecting to see healings and miracles. The throng blocked entrance into the already packed room. The determination of the men is seen in the fact that **they uncovered the roof** over the room

40	ªLuke 5:12–14
41	ªLuke 7:13
42	ªMatt. 15:28
44	ªLev. 14:1–32
45	ªLuke 5:15
	ᵇMark 2:2, 13; 3:7
	CHAPTER 2
1	ªMatt. 9:1
3	ªMatt. 4:24; 8:6
7	ªIs. 43:25
9	ªMatt. 9:5
12	ª[Phil. 2:11]
13	ªMatt. 9:9

where Jesus was preaching. The roof was probably flat and constructed of tiles laid one on another. **2:5 their faith:** Not only did the four men have faith, but the paralytic himself had it too. When Jesus announced to him, **your sins are forgiven,** He was implicitly acknowledging the paralytic's trust that He was the Messiah. **2:6, 7** Mark notes the opposition of **the scribes,** who under their breath accused Jesus of blasphemy. In Christ's day the scribes were commonly called lawyers. **2:9–11** Jesus asked the **which is easier** question to demonstrate the truth of His claim to forgive the man's sins—something only God can accomplish. Anyone could assert the ability to forgive sins, since there was no earthly way of confirming the statement. But to say **arise, take up your bed and walk** to a paralytic could be tested immediately by whether he walked or not. By healing the paralytic, Jesus made His pronouncement of forgiveness far more credible. **Son of Man** is a term regularly used for the Messiah (see 8:31; Dan. 7:13). **2:12 were amazed and glorified God:** The crowd's reaction showed that they understood the significance of Jesus' miracle. It is possible that some scribes and Pharisees joined in the acclamation. But permanent, life-changing faith is what Christ sought, not temporary adoration from the crowd. **2:13** Jesus regularly taught the multitudes in retreat settings. This is indicated by the continuous tense of the verbs

12. In the study note at the bottom of the page of the study Bible, you find a comment on Mark's statement that Jesus was "moved with compassion" for this leper: "He not only healed but touched the leper." Thus, you have learned that Jesus'

compassion for this leper was so strong that he healed him by touch, thus defiling himself ceremonially according to the dictates of the Jewish law. This healing was motivated by Jesus' love and compassion for a social outcast.

Certainly you will note some overlap of information among these various reference books, but by consulting all of them you will have gained a comprehensive understanding of the subject.

Conclusion

This exercise should have convinced you of the value of using *Strong's* with other study aids to cultivate greater understanding of the Bible. The simple steps outlined throughout this booklet have shown you how to get the most from your *Strong's Concordance*. Now that you know how to do this type of Bible study, the next step is up to you. Gather all your resources and put them to work as you learn more about God's Word.

Many of Nelson's reference works, including the *New Strong's*™ *Concordance*, are now available in electronic format. In addition to saving space, a CD-ROM enables you to research with ease and economy of time. The *Nelson's Electronic Bible Reference*™ *Library* (Professional Edition) provides some 76 Bible study resources on two disks.

Joy and grace to you as you study with *Strong's* "to show thyself approved unto God, a workman that needeth not to be ashamed, rightly dividing the word of truth" (2 Tim. 2:15).

More than $50 of Savings Coupons!
Build your reference library and save!

The New Strong's™ Exhaustive Concordance of the Bible (Comfort Print Edition)

$3.00 OFF

Not valid in combination with any other offer.

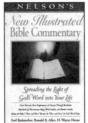

Nelson's New Illustrated Bible Commentary

$3.00 OFF

Not valid in combination with any other offer.

Nelson's New Illustrated Bible Manners & Customs

$3.00 OFF

Not valid in combination with any other offer.

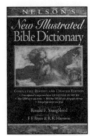

Nelson's New Illustrated Bible Dictionary

$3.00 OFF

Not valid in combination with any other offer.

Nelson's Electronic Bible Reference™ Library (Professional Edition)

$15.00 OFF

Not valid in combination with any other offer.

Nelson's Electronic Bible Reference™ Library (Deluxe Edition)

$10.00 OFF

Not valid in combination with any other offer.

Nelson's Electronic LESSONWORKS (Regular Edition)

$5.00 OFF

Not valid in combination with any other offer.

Nelson's Electronic LESSONWORKS (Deluxe Edition)

$10.00 OFF

Not valid in combination with any other offer.

Redeemable at your local bookstore.
Retailer— Return coupon for credit adjustment of net value to:
Nelson Reference Marketing
P. O. Box 141000
Nashville, TN 37214
Please include store name, address, and account #.

ISBN 078521438-0

9 780785 214380

Redeemable at your local bookstore.
Retailer— Return coupon for credit adjustment of net value
Nelson Reference Marketing
P. O. Box 141000
Nashville, TN 37214
Please include store name, address, and account #.

ISBN 084072072-6

9 780840 720726

Redeemable at your local bookstore.
Retailer— Return coupon for credit adjustment of net value to:
Nelson Reference Marketing
P. O. Box 141000
Nashville, TN 37214
Please include store name, address, and account #.

ISBN 084072071-8

9 780840 720719

Redeemable at your local bookstore.
Retailer— Return coupon for credit adjustment of net value t
Nelson Reference Marketing
P. O. Box 141000
Nashville, TN 37214
Please include store name, address, and account #.

ISBN 078521194-2

9 780785 211945

Redeemable at your local bookstore.
Retailer— Return coupon for credit adjustment of net value to:
Nelson Reference Marketing
P. O. Box 141000
Nashville, TN 37214
Please include store name, address, and account #.

ISBN 078521300-7

9 780785 213000

Redeemable at your local bookstore.
Retailer— Return coupon for credit adjustment of net value tc
Nelson Reference Marketing
P. O. Box 141000
Nashville, TN 37214
Please include store name, address, and account #.

ISBN 078521238-8

9 780785 212386

Redeemable at your local bookstore.
Retailer— Return coupon for credit adjustment of net value to:
Nelson Reference Marketing
P. O. Box 141000
Nashville, TN 37214
Please include store name, address, and account #.

ISBN 078520994-8

9 780785 209942

Redeemable at your local bookstore.
Retailer— Return coupon for credit adjustment of net value to:
Nelson Reference Marketing
P. O. Box 141000
Nashville, TN 37214
Please include store name, address, and account #.

ISBN 078521375-9

9 780785 213758